Designing your We
to Use Less Ener

Table of Contents

Table of Contents

Designing your Website to Use Less Energy

Designing your Website to Use Less Energy

Introduction

If you create websites and if you want to save energy, this book is for you. This book will explain how to design and code your website to use less energy when users browse it. So, if a lot of users are browsing you're website that will save a lot of energy.

Quick, get more users!

I call websites which save energy, Green Energy Websites.

I'm available for consulting on this subject. I also offer certification for your Green Energy Website. Contact me at https://stubbart.com.

Green Energy Websites are created by using more renewable energy and by speeding up your website to load faster (thus using less energy). In other words, by performance.

Color choices can also help, but are not a huge factor.

And, if you're making your website green, you'll also want to guide how it prints, so that it takes less ink to print it.

Introduction

In addition to making your websites save energy, you can also make some changes to how you develop websites and to how you browse the web which will save energy.

I explain each of these steps in detail, making them as simple as possible.

Designing your Website to Use Less Energy

Chapter 1 – Choosing a Webhost

The first requirement for a website to use less energy (for designing a Green Energy Website) is to host it with a Webhost which uses alternative energy. Most Green Energy Webhosts buy Renewable Energy Credits to offset their energy use.

The second requirement is for a Webhost to load pages quickly. Webhosts accomplish this partly by having multiple (mirror) servers for the webpages to load from. That way, they can load from the server closest to the user. However, there may not be information readily available on the average page load speed, so it's hard to rate providers on page load speed.

You'll also want to choose a Webhost that is up at least 97% of the time. This percentage is sometimes called uptime.

Look for a Webhost which offers services such as modPageSpeed and CloudFlare which may make your page load faster. Most Webhosts offer modPageSpeed, but some are going away from it as it makes some pages load slower.

Chapter 1 – Choosing a Webhost

I use modPageSpeed on all my websites and it makes them load faster, so it's worth a try. Dreamhost is switching from modPageSpeed to some new features on their Apache Servers. No word yet on when that switch will take place.

You may have to start a conversation with a webhost to find out some of this information.

Here are the top green Webhosts in terms of alternative energy.

US Webhost	Link
Dreamhost	http://www.dreamhost.com/
Aiso	http://www.aiso.net
GreenGeeks	https://www.greengeeks.com
InvisibleGold	http://invisiblegold.com/
GoGreen Hosting	http://www.gogreenhosting.com/
PlanetMind	http://www.planetmind.net/
Canada Webhost	**Link**
EthicalHosting	https://www.ethicalhost.ca

Designing your Website
to Use Less Energy

Dreamhost's Green information can be found at https://www.dreamhost.com/company/were-green/. Dreamhost's average page loading speed is 3.05 seconds/page. Anything under 5 seconds is very fast. Dreamhost offers modPageSpeed and CloudFlare.

Aiso's Green information can be found at http://www.aiso.net/company-vision.html and at http://www.aiso.net/technology-network-water.html. No information on page load speed or up-time was readily available. Looks like Aiso offers modPageSpeed and CloudFlare.

GreenGeeks' Green information can be found at https://www.greengeeks.com/about/. GreenGeek generates enough energy that they can meet their energy needs and put 6MW of energy per year back on the power grid. No information on page load speed or up-time was readily available. Looks like GreenGeeks offers modPageSpeed and CloudFlare.

InvisibleGold's Green information can be found at http://invisiblegold.com/About/environment/. No information on page load speed or up-time was readily available. No information was available on whether they offer modPageSpeed and CloudFlare or not.

GoGreenHosting's Green information can be found on the front page of their website at http://www.gogreenhosting.com/ and at http://www.gogreenhosting.com/environment/index.PHP. No information on page load speed or up-time was readily available. No information was available on whether they offer modPageSpeed or not. Looks like they probably offer CloudFlare.

Chapter 1 – Choosing a Webhost

PlanetMind's Green information can be found on the front page of their website at http://www.planetmind.net/. No information on page load speed or up-time was readily available. No information was available on whether they offer modPageSpeed or not. Looks like they probably offer CloudFlare.

Ethical Hosting's Green information can be found at https://www.ethicalhost.ca/renewable-energy-hosting.html. No information on page load speed or up-time was readily available. No information was available on whether they offer modPageSpeed or not. Looks like they offer CloudFlare.

Chapter 2 – Performance

Overview

The faster your webpage loads, the less energy it takes. And, the faster it loads, the more likely a user will stay at your site longer. Faster loading pages also help your ranking on search engines (SEO).

You can test your websites performance with Google Pagespeed Insights at https://developers.google.com/speed/pagespeed/insights/.
The insights returned will tell you things you can do to make your webpage load faster. The insights do not tell you just how fast your webpage loaded.

You will probably not want to follow all the recommendations. But you should consider following the top recommendations.

Yslow[1] and Firebug for Firefox[2] are the most recommended website performance checkers. But they're not necessarily the easiest to understand.

---

[1] YSlow http://yslow.org

Chapter 2 – Performance

Online tools which I find easier to understand and which tell me just how fast a webpage loads are available from:

- Pingdom at http://tools.pingdom.com/fpt/. My page loads in 1.97 seconds.
- WebpageTest at http://www.webpagetest.org/. My page loads in 2.72 seconds.
- Monitis at http://www.monitis.com/pageload/ In US 2.39s, in EU 2.98s, in Asia 4.04s.
- WebsiteOptimization Webpage Analyzer at http://www.websiteoptimization.com/services/analyze/ 2.29s on cable (T1)

The times from all these services for my website vary. They're all under 3 seconds (not counting the Asia time). You may want to take the average load time.

Most references place the pageload threshold at 5 seconds, some go as high as 10 minutes.

WebsiteOptimization Webpage Analyzer's analysis at the bottom of the results page told what their page speed tool was analyzing in addition to timing the website. It also gave some guidelines for some upper limits, such as Total HTML Size of 50K.

They place the pageload threshold at both 10 seconds and at 3-4 seconds. So their guidelines may not be consistent or accurate. But that's better than no guidelines at all, which is what you might get from other performance monitor sites.

An article from GoGreenHost[3] (different from GoGreenHosting Webhost), explains some of the

---

[2] Firebug http://getfirebug.com/
[3] GoGreenHost webpage performance article

Designing your Website
to Use Less Energy

performance issues. But they do not explain these issues as detailed or as clearly as I do in this book. (IMHO)

The steps below are listed in the order of importance in terms of saving energy. Those marked with *** are extremely important. Those not marked with *** are more optional and can be incorporated into your website as it makes sense to do so.

Chapter 2 – Performance

Step 1 – Upgrade your Website ***

Update your website to the latest version of HTML – HTML5 at the time of this writing. If you're using a Javascript Library, upgrade to the latest version. Same for PHP and Wordpress versions. Upgrade any other plug-ins, languages, and services you use on your website.

All that upgrading will make your website load faster, not to mention more secure, not to mention able to use more bells and whistles.

Your website should work similarly on all major browsers. Over 50% of the browsers used are Chrome or Android. Internet Explorer (IE) browsers are at 13% as is Firefox. Firefox is at 10%, Opera at 5%, and all others combined are at 8%.[4]

You may want to include Opera while testing to see that your websites work. Safari and Chrome are almost tied for mobile/tablet browsers.[5] You can probably ignore all other browsers.

---

[4] Wikipedia Browser Usage Stats
https://en.wikipedia.org/wiki/Usage_share_of_web_browsers
[5] NetMarketShare Mobile/Tablet Browser Usage Stats
https://www.netmarketshare.com/browser-market-

Designing your Website
to Use Less Energy

Some extra care and coding is needed to make sure that different browsers display your website correctly. Most of that extra coding was needed for IE for versions 8 and below. Now, only 13% of browsers are IE8 and only 8% are IE9.[6] So, your website can shed some of that extra code.

W3Counter[7] says only 2% of the browsers are IE9 and gives no statistics for IE8. So, you might also consider removing code directed at IE8 and IE9. That will slim down your website and make it load faster.

Can I Use[8] tells you which features can be used on which browsers – make sure to read the Notes and Known Issues at the bottom of the page for that feature. To speed things up, you can omit prefixes needed for browsers which are not used much – IE9 and earlier, Opera, and Opera Mini. Safari is usually not rated as having a high usage, but usage is high (perhaps highest) for mobile users since Safari is Apple and there are a lot of Apple iPhones out there.

Hovering over a browser version in Can I Use will show their estimate of its usage. To see the total percentage for a browser, you'd need to add up the percentage for all versions. However, looking at percentages might help you decide which versions of a browser you want to support.

For instance. IE10 is only used by 1.02% of users. So you may want to omit that version also. You may want to go all the way back to Chrome version 44. Or you can

---

share.aspx?qprid=1&qpcustomb=1
[6] NetMarketShare Browser Usage Stats
https://www.netmarketshare.com/browser-market-share.aspx?qprid=2&qpcustomd=0
[7] W3Counter Browser Usage Stats
http://www.w3counter.com/globalstats.PHP
[8] Can I Use http://caniuse.com/

Chapter 2 – Performance

assume that most users will be upgrading to the latest version soon enough, possibly before you get your website published, and just code for that version. (Or you may want to start by supporting the latest versions of the most popular browsers and add extra support over time.)

Tutorials Point tells which HTML tags and attributes have been deprecated in HTML5[9]. Browsers may still interpret them correctly. You may want to upgrade before they're not supported.

W3Schools shows which browsers support which CSS3 options.[10]

---

[9] Tutorials Point – HTML5 Deprecated Tags
http://www.tutorialspoint.com/html5/html5_deprecated_tags.htm
[10] CSS3 option support by Browser
http://www.w3schools.com/cssref/css3_browsersupport.asp

Designing your Website to Use Less Energy

Step 2 – Limit External Feeds ***

External Feeds come from Ads, RSS Feeds, Affiliate Links, and other services like Google Translate. Consider limiting ads to three to a page. Also consider if the ads are making you money or if they are just making money for the advertisers. If Ads load from different sources, consider limiting the number of sources. If your ads do not load quickly, consider changing sources.

Affiliate Links tend to load faster than ads and tend to pay better. Also your chances of finding green Affiliate Links are higher that your chances of finding Green Ads.

If you're using a slower loading service like Google Translate or Facebook Like, try to load those services after the rest of your page loads. See Step 5 – Lighten your Javascript ***.

Special fonts and other items imported through `<link>` tags or `@import` CSS commands are also considered external feeds. Consider limiting them.

Chapter 2 – Performance

Most browsers will load at least 6 six files at the same time, including the file of your webpage. Try to keep the number of external files to 5.

For more information on speeding up the loading of Services and Plug-ins see Chapter 3 – Plug-ins and Other Services.

Designing your Website to Use Less Energy

Step 3 – Replace Flash ***

Adobe Flash kills batteries on laptops and smartphones. Flash can load slowly. And there have been several security issues with it. Apple and Android Smartphones do not support Flash.[11] I suspect the reason Flash uses lots of energy and kills batteries, is because it's usually set to constantly loop, rather than loop once on demand.

Replace Flash with HTML5 Canvas and Javascript or some other method. Only 10% of websites use Flash, so yours is probably not one of them.

HTML5 provides the `<canvas>` tag for drawing objects.
```
<canvas id="mydrawing" width="300"
height="200"></canvas>
```
Remember, for your webpage to be considered HTML5, it should start with `<!DOCTYPE html>`.

---

[11] Flash Update: Browsers are now supporting Flash again, so long as it's called through PPAPI (Pepper Plugin API (Application Programming Interface)) or NaCl (Native Client) rather than through NPAPI (Netscape Plugin API). This applies to other plugins as well including Adobe Reader and Java.
https://www.chromium.org/nativeclient/getting-started/getting-started-background-and-basics; https://www.chromium.org/developers/npapi-deprecation

Chapter 2 – Performance

Drawing images with HTML5 Canvas, requires knowing some trigonometry. The more complex the image, the more trigonometry is required. Drawing simple squares, adding rounded corners, adding text, coloring the text are all fairly simple. Drawing lines that are not horizontal or vertical and drawing curves (other than rounded corners on squares) can quickly get complex.

You pass parameters to Javascript functions to draw the object on the canvas. The parameters are in coordinates (from the top-left corner, rather than bottom-left or center-center), and in radians (rather than degrees).

Luckily, there is help in the form of Javascript Libraries. (They will add to your page load speed. So choose a light-weight one.) Most of the libraries only simplify the number of steps and perhaps combine parameters. Or they use a different syntax which doesn't simplify much. They typically don't simplify the trigonometry although some claim to by using vector math instead.

jsDraw2DX from jsFiction simplifies the trigonometry and the number of parameters. Basically you tell it where you want to start drawing, what you want to draw (rectangle, lines, circle, curve, etc), and the size of what you want to draw. It figures out the rest. It still keeps functions for the more complex curves like Bezier, but also adds a simple drawCurve function. You simply pass points you want to be included in the curve to drawCurve. It's helpful to understand HTML5 Canvas basics in order to understand jsDraw2DX.

So, back to HTML5 Canvas.

The canvas tag needs three attributes – ID, Width, and Height. You can give it a border via CSS.

Designing your Website to Use Less Energy

The canvas tag does nothing by itself. Javascript uses the canvas ID to manipulate the canvas so that it ends up being a drawing.

You can use Javascript to draw shapes on the canvas, place images on the canvas, draw text on the canvas, or do any combination of those things. You can combine drawings, give your drawings transparency, use gradients, animate your drawings, add shadows, make your text look like outline text, give your text depth, etc.

The basic Javascript for a canvas tag with `id="mydrawing"` is

```
<script>
canvas = document.getElementById('mydrawing');
context = canvas.getContext('2d');
// do something with the context
</script>
```

1) First, get the canvas element via the id – `getElementById`.
2) Second, get the context of the canvas – `getContext`. 2d says, use the 2-dimensional context. Keep reading for 3-dimensional context.
3) Then do something with the context.
   a) Set the starting point or origin of the drawing by `context.moveTo(x,y)`, `context.fillText('Hello World!', x, y)`, `context.strokeText('Hello World!', x, y)`, `context.drawImage(imageObj, x, y, width, height)`, or a similar method which specifies the origin. The x, y coordinates of 0,0 specify the top-left corner of the canvas. 0,width specify the top-right corner. 0,height specify the bottom-left corner. width,height specify the bottom-right corner.
   b) Manipulate the drawing, adding more lines or segments, filling the drawing with a color, adding transformations etc.

Chapter 2 – Performance

    c) Finalize your drawing, via `stroke`, `fill`, `filltext`, `drawimage`, `stroketext`, `wraptext`, or similar method. Note: Sometimes setting the origin, manipulating the drawing, and finalizing the drawing is all done by finalizing the drawing.

4) Finish your drawing by repeating steps 1, 2, and 3 as needed to draw multiple objects on the canvas.

To clear the canvas to start over or during an animation, use:
```
context.clearRect(0, 0, canvas.width,
canvas.height);
```

See more on animation in Chapter 3 – Plug-ins and Other Services Animation.

The best tutorial for working with the HTML5 canvas is the HTML5 Canvas Tutorial by Eric Rodwell[12] with an accompanying reference page[13].

W3 Schools offers overview pages[14] with an accompanying reference page[15].

DiveIntoHTML also offers a tutorial[16]. It suggests resetting the canvas by setting `canvas.width=canvas.width`. The `context.clearRect` method mentioned above is the preferred method, meaning it clears the canvas better. This

---

[12] HTML5 Canvas Tutorial
http://www.html5canvastutorials.com/advanced/html5-canvas-linear-motion-animation/
[13] HTML5 Canvas Tutorial Ref
http://cheatsheetworld.com/programming/html5-canvas-cheat-sheet/
[14] W3Schools Canvas Overview
http://www.w3schools.com/html/html5_canvas.asp
[15] W3Schools Canvas Overview Ref
http://www.w3schools.com/tags/ref_canvas.asp
[16] DiveIntoHTML Canvas Tutorial
http://diveintohtml5.info/canvas.html

Designing your Website
to Use Less Energy

tutorial also explains how to make sure your lines fit inside your canvas, by taking into consideration the line width and height.

Chapter 2 – Performance

webgl

Once you've got a good handle on using canvas to draw 2-dimensional drawings, you can try your hand at 3-dimensional canvas drawings.

To draw 3-dimensional canvas objects, your basic Javascript would look like this:

```
<script>
var canvas = document.getElementById('mydrawing');
var context = canvas.getContext('webgl');
// do something with the context
</script>
```

Notice the context is webgl and not 3d. webgl is based on OpenGL which is an API for drawing 2-dimensional and 3-dimensional objects.

If you have questions about webgl which the webgl references below don't answer, try using this OpenGL reference[17] to answer them.

After setting the context, you create a drawing buffer which contains a color, depth, and a stencil buffer. The depth buffer controls the third dimension. The stencil

---

[17] OpenGL reference https://www.khronos.org/opengl/

Designing your Website
to Use Less Energy

buffer controls which fragments of the image are drawn and which aren't.

If you resize the canvas (change width or height), set the viewport as follows:

```
mydrawing.viewport(0, 0,
mydrawing.drawingBufferWidth,
mydrawing.drawingBufferHeight);
```

HTML5 Rocks has a webgl Tutorial[18]. This tutorial assumes you know what you're doing. But is still a good reference.

If you're going to use webgl, you might want to use the Pixi.js Javascript library http://www.pixijs.com/. This is a lightweight library which may make webgl (3d) drawings easier to draw.

Information on webgl is available from Khronos[19] – the makers. Reference starts on that page at DOM Interfaces[20].

---

[18] HTML5 Rocks webgl Tutorial
http://www.html5rocks.com/en/tutorials/webgl/webgl_fundamentals/
[19] Khronos webgl info
https://www.khronos.org/webgl/wiki/Main_Page
[20] Khronos webgl ref
https://www.khronos.org/registry/webgl/specs/1.0/#5

Chapter 2 – Performance

Step 4 – Lighten your Images ***

For images to work on the web, they need to be in JPG, GIF, or PNG formats. Images should be compressed. They should also have a resolution of 72 pixels/inch. Compression and lower resolution will result in faster load times for the image.

Different people have different opinions on the best image size. If the image will be a fixed size on the screen, I save the image at that size. Larger images will need to be resized for smaller screens.

I find a maximum size of 3x4 inches (216x288 pixels) works well for most situations. Facebook prefers 400x400 pixels. Twitter prefers 120x120 pixels. Facebook and Twitter both prefer square images in their posts.

Preload your images. The following Javascript code will preload an webpage. Load each image on your webpage whether it's in HTML, Javascript, or CSS (or other). You can get all the images in your HTML with

```
imgs=document.getElementsByTagName('img').
```

However, they will not be available until your page is loaded and by then, it's too late to preload them.

Designing your Website
to Use Less Energy

Place this code right after the `<body>` tag.

```
// preload images in HTML, Javascript, and CSS
(and other), one image at a time
  preload_image("x.jpg")
  preload_image("...")

  //preload the image...
  function preload_image(myimg) {
  if (document.images)
  {
      pic1= new Image(300,400); /* width,height - no
parameters are needed if your images are optimized */
      pic1.src=myimg;
  }
  }
```

If you're loading a whole gallery of images, you may want to use a function from Mark Meyer Photography[21] which loads the images into an array.

You can also use the Javascript Libraries preloadimages.js or preloadr.js.[22]

img-resize, Smush.it, Shrink Pictures, and Simple Image Optimizer[23] will resize your images for you.

---

[21] Mark Meyer gallery load http://www.photo-mark.com/notes/image-preloading/

[22] preloadimages.js https://github.com/bahamas10/preloadimages.js; preloadr.js https://github.com/borisschapira/preloadr

[23] img-resize http://img-resize.com/; Smush.it http://www.imgopt.com/; Shrink Pictures http://www.shrinkpictures.com/; Simple Image Optimizer http://www.simpleimageresizer.com/image-optimizer

Chapter 2 – Performance

Sprites

If you have lots of images, you can try to use sprites.

I have not found sprites to be simple. So I'm just including some basics here in case you want to try them.

A sprite is a png image which combines many images into one picture/file. You may be able to use a gif image rather than a png image.

The sprite image is then displayed as a background image. The portion of the image you want to display is set by using CSS `background-position`, `background-size`, `width`, and `height` settings.

There are simpler methods for getting your images to display faster, than using sprites. Sprites should be considered, if you're using lots and lots of images. Sprites are more suited to images with transparent backgrounds such as icons, happy faces, etc.

You might be able to use HTML5 Canvas or SVG[24] to display your sprites more easily (and accurately).

---

[24] Sprites with HTML5 Canvas
http://www.williammalone.com/articles/create-html5-canvas-

Designing your Website
to Use Less Energy

First, you need to size your image to be the same size as the final size you want or at least to be proportional to the final size you want. Making your individual images the final size will slightly speed up your website. But it may mean more work than it's worth.

You may also run into issues with sprites if you resize your images based on browser size (media size). And, you may not want your image to be a background image.

Sprite CSS looks something like this:
```
.sprite_img_1, .sprite_img_2, .sprite_img_3
{display: inline-block; background:
url('sprite_main.png') no-repeat; overflow: hidden;
text-indent: -9999px; text-align: left;}
   /* use background-size to resize image */
   .sprite_img_1 { background-position: -2px -0px;
width: 252px; height: 144px; }
   .sprite_img_2 { background-position: -2px -146px;
width: 239px; height: 238px; }
   .sprite_img_3 { background-position: -2px -386px;
width: 150px; height: 163px; }
```

`background-position` is from the left, top of the sprite image.

There are some online sprite generators[25] which can help. These typically take all your images, place them in a sprite png and give you the corresponding CSS.

---

javascript-sprite-animation/; Sprites with SVG
http://www.sitepoint.com/use-svg-image-sprites/

[25] Online sprite generators: CSSsprites http://CSS.spritegen.com/; Sprite Pad http://wearekiss.com/spritepad; CSS Sprites Generator http://csssprites.com/; Instant Sprite http://instantsprite.com/; SpriteCow http://www.spritecow.com/; Retina CSS Sprite Generator http://www.retinaspritegenerator.com/; CSS Sprite Generator by {CSS} Portal http://www.cssportal.com/CSS-sprite-generator/.

Chapter 2 – Performance

If you add an image or resize an image, you need to go through the process all over again.

These generators typically download a zip file which contains both the sprite image file and the CSS file.

Designing your Website to Use Less Energy

Step 5 – Lighten your Javascript ***

If you're using Javascript for presentation, that is, if you're using Javascript to display something on your website, such as a menu which is the same on every page, then the Javascript needs to be executed where it needs to be displayed.

Document Presentation is usually accomplished by `document.write` or `id.innerHTML` where `id` is the id of an element on your page, such as a `<div>`.

Presentation Javascript is often written in a `<script>` tag where it needs to be executed in the webpage. For example:

```
<script>
document.write('Some text goes here');
</script>
```

You can place this Javascript in a function in your Javascript file and just execute the function where you want that part of your website displayed.

For example if you called your function `write_text`:

```
<script>
write_text();
</script>
```

Chapter 2 – Performance

Combine all your code into one Javascript file that is loaded in your webpage by a `<script src="…"></script>`, where the ellipses is the name of your Javascript file.

Most people suggest placing the `<script src="…"></script>` right before your `</body>` tag.
But that option doesn't always work if you have Presentation Javascript. You usually need to load your Javascript before it needs to be used for Presentation and before you need to reference anything from it.

Sometimes, especially if you have Presentation Javascript, you need to load it as early as possible, possibly even having the `<script src="…"></script>` in the `<head>` section of your webpage.

Keeping your Javascript file small will help it load quickly, no matter where it is loaded in your webpage.

If you Javascript which relies on the page being already loaded (as some jQuery scripts do), place that Javascript right before the `</body>` tag, unless there's a reason to place it early.

It is also recommended to use the `defer` and `async` attributes of the `<script>` statement, i.e. `<script src="…" defer></script>` and `<script src="…" async></script>`.
These attributes can only be used with external Javascript files. These delay loading your Javascript file until other things are loaded.

Using these options is not that simple. You'll want to try to use them if you're loading more than 6 Javascript files

.

Designing your Website
to Use Less Energy

(usually if you're using external Javascript libraries) or if one or more of your Javascript files is very large.

If you have `document.write` or any other statement which produces document output in your Javascript, that is if you have Presentation Javascript, do not use these options.

If the script does not rely on other scripts, use `async`. If it does, use `defer`.

Test to make sure all your functions load in the correct order.

`async` will pause your page loading to execute the Javascript when the Javascript has finished loading, but the Javascript may load at any time in the process of loading your webpage (it doesn't necessarily load where you have placed it). So it may load before another Javascript loads and not be available when you need it to be.

`defer` only executes the Javascript after the rest of your webpage has loaded. `defer` scripts load in the order that they appear in the document.

There is a bug in IE9 with `defer`. And browsers are changing the way they load `async` and `defer` scripts[26], so occasional retests are warranted.

JavascriptKit[27] offers a function for dynamically loading either CSS or Javascript files. This may be a simpler solution than `defer` or `async`.

HeadJS[28] can be used to help load Javascript without slowing down the load of your webpage.

---

[26] Chome changes how `async` and `defer` scripts are loaded http://thenextweb.com/apps/2015/03/18/google-uses-new-techniques-to-speed-up-javascript-load-times-in-latest-chrome-release/

[27] JavscriptKit function for dynamically loading CSS or Javascript files http://www.Javascriptkit.com/javatutors/loadJavascriptcss.shtml

Chapter 2 – Performance

You may want to minimize your Javascript by joining several lines into one (perhaps having one line per function) and removing whitespace. Remember to end each statement with a semi-colon (;) before joining lines.

You can minimize your Javascript further via the Closure Compiler[29]. The simple option is the best. The advanced option may minimize your code to the point where it is not useable.

You can also minimize your code using the Javascript Minifier[30].

Until you get used to reading minimized code, keep an un-minimized version of your Javascript which you can easily maintain and re-minimize.

Other languages beside Javascript are used in websites. The most popular websites use C, Go, Java, Python, Dart, PHP, Hack, Erlang, D, Perl, Scala, Ruby on Rails, and ASP.

Other languages used by these websites include Django – a Python Framework; Hack – a PHP dialect developed by Facebook which performs faster than native PHP; and Xhp – an extension of PHP mainly for XML.

Javascript, PHP, and Ruby on Rails are the languages which are most accessible to the majority of website developers.

Make sure you're using the latest (or a recent) version of the language.

---

[28] HeadJS http://headjs.com/; Exis Article about HeadJS http://exisweb.net/web-site-optimization-making-javascript-load-faster
[29] Closure Compile http://closure-compiler.appspot.com/home
[30] Javascript Minifier http://Javascript-minifier.com/

Designing your Website to Use Less Energy

Use built-in functions and commands, rather than writing your own code to do the same thing.

Keep the code short but maintainable.

Your webhost may offer more ways to speed up these languages.

Consider switching your Javascript front-end code to back-end code – probably PHP or Python, possibly Ruby. Switching to back-end allows the server to run the code, rather than the user's computer/browser. And that should be faster.

It might be easier to switch to a server-side Javascript solution like Node.js. Node.js offers server side Javascript-like solutions. It still runs some code as straight Javascript, so you may not gain what you'd hoped in terms of speed.

If you have lots of contiguous `document.write` statements in your Javascript (or perhaps a `document.write` statement in a loop), build a string and reduce all these to one `document.write` statement. This will speed up your website, though it may not be noticeable unless you have many `document.write` statements.

You can also add a Javascript function to execute `document.write` for you: `d_w(x){document.write(x)}`.

This will reduce the size of your Javascript file and make it load faster. However that extra step to call the function to do the `document.write` may cancel out any speed increase you gained. It will however save you typing time.

If you have lots of inline Javascript, you can try to speed up the load by placing each section of Javascript in a function.

Chapter 2 – Performance

Place `windows.onload=a();`, where the function is `a`, right after the function.

This will defer loading the Javascript until the rest of your page has loaded.

However, your page may be loading slowly due to having lots of document.write statements, rather than because you have lots of inline Javascript. See the previous paragraph for speeding up `document.write`.

Rather than placing `arr.length` in your `for` statement, assign it to a variable just before the `for` statement.

If you're using jQuery or another Javascript Library (Framework), see jQuery and Other Javascript Libraries (Frameworks) for more information on speeding up your website.

Designing your Website to Use Less Energy

Step 6 – Lighten your CSS
***

W3Counter[31] shows the most common display sizes. You'll want to make your CSS handle at least the following screen sizes:

	Screen Width in Pixels
Large Screen (Laptop or Larger)	> 600
Small Screen	481-600
Tablet	321-480
Small Phone	1-320

If you're designing special applications for web glasses (Google glass is basically no longer supported) or web watches, you need to have CSS to handle those devices. You'll also want CSS for printing.

---

[31] http://www.w3counter.com/globalstats.PHP

Chapter 2 – Performance

It is recommended to place all your CSS into one file. I prefer to limit it to 2 files (Screen and Print). The Screen and Print CSS files contain all the CSS specifications. This way, I'm certain I've set everything I need to.

(My print CSS contains a few less for hidden elements which will never print. It also contains a `.noprint` class which can be used to not print various elements by setting `display:none`.)

The Screen CSS includes Large Screen, Small Screen, Tablet, and Small Phone variations to the CSS. Place all your CSS in either the Large Screen or Small Phone section and only the variations to that CSS which are specific to those devices, statements which reduce/enlarge the size of elements and fonts, in the other section.

Use the media statement to separate sections:
`@media screen and (max-width: ###px) {...}`

Load CSS files/sections in descending/ascending order by width, followed by the CSS Print file.

Don't forget to include
`<meta name="viewport" content="width=device-width, initial-scale=1.0" />`
in your HTML `<head>` section to allow the browser to scale to the device.

Then in your CSS specify `html, body {max-width: 100vw;}`. This sets the maximum width of your website to 100vw, where 1vw = 1% of the viewport width (just set by `<meta name="viewport">`). In other words, the maximum width of your website is the maximum width of the device.

You may also want to use `em` (basically 1 character wide and high in the current font size) rather than `px` (pixels) for small measurements. Use `vw` (1% viewport width) or `vh` (1% viewport height) for large measurements.

Designing your Website
to Use Less Energy

You can also use `vmin` (minimum viewport size (width or height). `vmax` is not supported by IE.

Remove all `style=` statements from your HTML elements. Place all styling in your CSS stylesheet, referencing the element type, class, or ID.

Once you have all your CSS in external files, minimize it by joining lines – 1 line per element, class, or id. You can reduce your CSS more by joining even more lines and removing spaces where possible.

Your CSS can be minimized by using the CSS Minifier at http://cssminifier.com/.

Keep an unminimized or less minimized version of your CSS which you can read.

Smashing Magazine[32] sets a limit of 14KB for the HTML and CSS of each webpage for their site. They place the CSS elements which are displayed in the top part of their page (first 800`px` height-wise) in a `<style>` tag in the `<head>` section of their webpage. The rest of the CSS is displayed with Javascript after the rest of the page loads.

Alternately, you may want to place the common CSS in your external CSS file, and page specific CSS in a `<style>` tag.

Both of these methods require lots of work to get everything organized. Being organized is great. But there may be simpler ways to speed up your website.

JavascriptKit offers a function for dynamically loading either CSS or Javascript files[33].

---

[32] Smashing Magazine webpage guidelines
http://www.smashingmagazine.com/2014/09/improving-smashing-magazine-performance-case-study/

Chapter 2 – Performance

If you're website has been around a while, you probably have CSS classes that you no longer use. If they're causing your CSS file to be much larger than needed, consider identifying them and removing them. See Appendix A: Remove unused CSS classes from stylesheet for assistance in doing so.

Check Can I Use, What CSS to Prefix, and Autoprefixer[34] to see which CSS prefixes (-webkit, -ms) you need, if any.

---

[33] JavascriptKit function to dynamically load external file
http://www.Javascriptkit.com/javatutors/loadJavascriptcss.shtml
[34] Can I Use http://caniuse.com/; What CSS to Prefix
http://shouldiprefix.com/; Autoprefixer
https://github.com/postcss/autoprefixer

Designing your Website
to Use Less Energy

Step 7 – Lighten your Frameworks ***

If you're using a PHP or Javascript Framework consider using a lighter one. Most frameworks are fast by design, only requesting updated information from the server.

Fast lightweight PHP frameworks are Phalcon and Slim[35]. Fast Javascript Frameworks are Backbone, Angular, React, JSBlocks and Node[36].

Your page may load faster if you skip the framework altogether. See Chapter 3 – Plug-ins and Other Services jQuery and Other Javascript Libraries (Frameworks) for more information.

---

[35] Phalcon PHP Framework https://phalconphp.com/en/; Slim PHP Framework http://www.slimframework.com/

[36] Backbone Javascript Framework http://backbonejs.org/; Angular Javascript Framework https://angularjs.org/; React Javscript Framework https://facebook.github.io/react/; JSBlocks Javascript Framework http://jsblocks.com/; Node Javascript Framework https://nodejs.org/en/

Chapter 2 – Performance

Step 8 – Reduce the number of Elements on your Webpage

***

Run the following code on your Webpage to find out the number of HTML elements (tags) on your webpage. Place the code below the `<body>` tag. Remember to comment the code after testing.

```
<script>alert(document.getElementsByTagName('*').length);</script>
```

Try to get the number of elements to be under 700. The easiest way to reduce the number of elements is to split the page into multiple pages.

If your page is too long or has too much information on it, chances are people won't spend much time looking at it, unless it's very interesting reading.

Designing your Website to Use Less Energy

Step 9 – Check your Database Queries ***

If you have database queries on your website, make sure they perform well. If possible, reduce the number of database queries.

For MySQL, the most popular database for websites, use `Visual Explain Current Statement` in the MySQL Workbench[37] to help explain slow queries.

Add indexes to tables as needed. (Small table do not need indexes. Indexes will make them slower. Test with explain to see if your table qualifies as small.) Use indexes in the `WHERE` clause of your query.

You can adjust system variables[38] to improve performance. I consider this an advanced option because you can just as easily degrade performance.

Use `LIMIT` and `OFFSET` to limit the number of rows returned from your query[39].

---

[37] MySQL Workbench
https://www.mysql.com/products/workbench/
[38] MySQL System Variables
http://dev.mysql.com/doc/refman/5.1/en/server-system-variables.html
[39] `LIMIT` and `OFFSET`
http://www.w3schools.com/PHP/PHP_mysql_select_limit.asp

Chapter 2 – Performance

Make sure to upgrade to at least version 5.5 which uses the INNODB storage engine by default. INNODB is faster with large tables.

Data can be stored and accessed by other means than databases. See Storing/Querying Data in Chapter 4 Make Your Own Add-in for more information. Some of these may be faster than a database, depending on your situation.

Designing your Website to Use Less Energy

Step 10 – Limit Iframes and Cookies

If you use Iframes or Cookies, try to reduce the number of Iframes and Cookies. They are useful, but can slow down your website.

If you're using `<iframe>` tags for Youtube Videos, consider a method by Digital Inspiration[40] for reducing their size. Videos can now use the `<video>` tag instead.[41] Audios can use the `<audio>` tag.[42] See Chapter 3 – Plug-ins and Other Services Video and Audio for more information.

See Storing/Querying Data in Chapter 4 Make Your Own Add-in for more information on Cookies.

---

[40] Digital Inspiration reduce Youtube Iframe size
http://www.labnol.org/internet/light-youtube-embeds/27941/

[41] `<video>` tag http://www.w3schools.com/tags/tag_video.asp

[42] `<audio>` tag http://www.w3schools.com/tags/tag_audio.asp

Step 11 – Div vs Table

There is a lot of chatter on the internet about switching from `<table>` to `<div>`. This is mostly to aid in helping your table display well on smaller devices. You may need to convert some tables to divs. If your table is small enough, it can remain a table. Many table attributes have been deprecated in HTML5 and need to be replaced with CSS.

Keep tables to under 100 elements.

Specify column widths as percents.

There are many ways to convert tables to divs. Make your divs easy to distinguish from each other, since the table, row, and cells will all be divs. This can be done with comments or classes.

The easiest method is to use CSS display table attributes. Replace `<table>` with `<div class="table">` having style `.table {display:table}`.
Replace `<tr>` with `<div class="table_row">` having style `.table_row {display:table-row}`.

Designing your Website
to Use Less Energy

Replace `<td>` with `<div class="table_cell">` having style `.table_cell {display:table-cell}`.

Often table rows can be removed when using this method.

If you use `<td valign="top">` specify `.table_cell {display:table-cell;vertical-align:top}`.

Another easy method for converting tables to divs is to use the CSS `flex` attribute. The problem with using flex is that you still need to add `-webkit` for recent versions of Safari(8) and `-ms` for recent versions of IE(10). `flex` is commonly used when you have a fixed width column and other columns which you want to grow to fill the available space. An example follows:

```
<div class="table">
<div class="col1">Column 1 Fixed Width</div>
<div class="col1">Column 2 Grow to Size</div>
</div>

. table {display: -webkit-flex; display: -ms-flex;
display: flex;}
. col1 { display:inline; float:left; width:204px;
}
. col2 { display:inline; float:left; -webkit-flex-
grow: 1; -ms-flex-positive: 1; flex-grow: 1; padding-
left:1em; max-width:400px;}
```

`-ms-flex-positive` is the equivalent of `flex-grow`. Specify `max-width` to ensure that your text will wrap in IE10 and IE11.

If you use `flex`, make sure and check the notes and known issues at Can I Use[43]. Workarounds are at Philip Walton Flexbugs.[44]

---

[43] Can I Use `flex` http://caniuse.com/#search=flex
[44] Philip Walton Flexbugs https://github.com/philipwalton/flexbugs

Chapter 2 – Performance

The most popular method of converting tables to divs is to use floating divs. Many examples will use `float:right` and list the table cell divs in reverse (right-to-left) order. I find it easier to use `float:left` and list the table cells in left-to-right order.

```
<div class="table">
<div class="col">
</div>
</div>
<div class="float_clear"></div>

.table {display:block;width:100%;}
.col
{display:inline;float:left;width:120px;height:380px;}
.float_clear {clear:both;}
```

`clear:both` clears (resets) all divs to not float. This is important if you display anything below your floating divs.

Designing your Website to Use Less Energy

Step 12 – Reduce Page to Itself

Remove any part of the page which does not pertain to this page. This includes CSS, Javascript, Links, etc. Just because you use something on most pages of your website, doesn't mean you need to include it on this page, if it is not used. This is especially important for large files.

Chapter 3 – Plug-ins and Services

Overview

There are several types of plug-ins, apps, and other services which are used on websites. These add-ins include:

- Content Management Systems (CMS) for building

    websites and for blogs

- jQuery and Other Javascript Libraries (Frameworks)

- Help for Navigating your Webpage

- Forms Management

- Social Sharing Buttons

- Maps and GPS

- External Feeds including RSS

- Photo Gallery Management

- Webstores, Shopping Carts, and Buy Buttons

- Chat

Designing your Website
to Use Less Energy

- Comments and Guestbook

- Search

- Event Calendars for Appointments and Scheduling

- Communities and Restricted Access (Members Only)

- Video and Audio

- Animation

- Weather

- Financial Info including Stocks

- Translation

- Special Fonts

- Other Plug-Ins

Some of these, especially CMS, can include multiple other plug-ins. The more plug-ins, apps, and other services a website has, the more slowly it will load and therefore the more energy it will take to load it.

Care should be taken to limit the number of these services and to lighten their load when they are used. Using the latest version will often help a service or plug-in load faster.

If you are already using a CMS or Framework like jQuery, choose lightweight plug-ins which are designed for that CMS or Framework.

Check your CMS or Framework for plug-ins. You can find which plug-ins are popular at BuiltWith[45] where they are called widgets. Most plug-ins are specific to a CMS,

---

[45] BuiltWith Widget Trends http://trends.builtwith.com/widgets

Chapter 3 – Plug-ins and Services

others can be easily used on websites (using it on CMS may take much more work), some have multiple versions for websites and various CMS, some have one version which works anywhere.

To determine which add-on is running fastest for your webhost and your configuration, create 2 new webpages. Make them new, so they're not already cached.

Upload them to a test area of your website – one that you've made off-limits to robots. For instance if you had a test directory/folder on your website call test, you would place a robots.txt text file in your main directory something like

```
User-agent: *
Disallow: /test
```

Determine the load speed of each page – see Chapter 2 – Performance Overview.

Sometimes plug-in code works faster than anything you could write and besides, if the code already exists and is fast enough, you might as well not reinvent the wheel. And sometimes they're not faster because they're trying to do a lot more or cover a lot more situations than you need to.

Plug-ins are available for most CMS. They are also available for jQuery, MooTools and other Javascript Libraries (Frameworks). You can find plug-ins for your website at Powr.io, I3DThemes, Wolfram Alpha, WidgetsCode, and 100Widgets.[46]

---

[46] Powr.io plug-ins https://www.powr.io/plugins; I3DThemes plug-ins http://www.i3dthemes.com/website-plugins/#view-plugins; Wolfram Alpha widgets http://www.wolframalpha.com/widgets/; WidgetsCode http://widgetscode.com/; 100Widgets http://100widgets.com/

Designing your Website
to Use Less Energy

If the Widgets use Flash you'll want to avoid them as Flash is quickly losing support and some browsers won't display it for security reasons.

Many widgets display ads on your website (at least with the free version). Ads will increase your energy usage and will often slow your page load.

Some plug-ins track what happens on your system, perhaps more than you would wish. Choose wisely and lightly.

Chapter 3 – Plug-ins and Services

Content Management Systems (CMS)

Content Management Systems are used to build websites. They can be used to build an entire website or just certain pages, such as the blog. The most popular CMS are Wordpress, Joomla, and Drupal[47].

Dreamhost offers suggestions for speeding up Wordpress[48]. Most of these performance improvements are achieved by installing plug-ins. Most of the plug-ins have to do with caching. Dreamhost has also created a faster premium version of Wordpress called Dreampress[49].

GreenGeeks say their WordPress is very fast.

Some of the suggestion for improving the speed of Wordpress (caching, resizing images, etc.) also apply to other CMS.

The Joomla Community Magazine offers tips for speeding up Joomla.[50] Joomla SEO compares various

---

[47] Wordpress https://wordpress.com/; Drupal https://www.drupal.org/; Joomla https://www.joomla.org/
[48] Speed up Wordpress http://wiki.dreamhost.com/Fine_Tuning_Your_WordPress_Install
[49] Dreampress https://www.dreamhost.com/hosting/wordpress/

Designing your Website
to Use Less Energy

Joomla Templates for performance.[51] They also offer the same performance tips as Joomla Community Magazine.

Drupal offers optimization tips.[52] You may want to switch to PressFlow[53] which is a distribution of Drupal designed for performance.

Other popular CMS are vBulletin, Google Blogger, ExpressionEngine, cPanel, DotNetNuke, Adobe Experience Manager, WPTouch for Wordpress (a CMS on top of a CMS), ModX, TextPattern, Refinery (a Ruby on Rails CMS), Concrete5, Umbraco, TinyCMS, GetSimpleCMS, and Pligg[54].

If you have the option of choosing which CMS you use, choose one that's easy to install, can do what you need it to (and what you may need it to do in the future), is easy to use, has been around long enough that you'll have good support, and which has great security and a small footprint.
For small footprint, consider one of those listed at vivalogo[55] (so long as it meets those criteria).

---

[50] Speed up Joomla http://magazine.joomla.org/issues/issue-apr-2014/item/1820-10-tips-for-a-fast-joomla-website
[51] Joomla template comparison http://joomlaseo.com/blog/templates-performance-comparison
[52] Drupal optimization tips https://www.drupal.org/node/1722250
[53] Pressflow http://www.pressflow.org/
[54] vBulletin http://www.vbulletin.com/; Blogger http://www.blogger.com/; Expression Engine – find at https://ellislab.com/; cPanel http://cpanel.com/; DotNetNuke http://www.dnnsoftware.com/; Adobe Experience Manager http://www.adobe.com/marketing-cloud/enterprise-content-management.html; WPTouch for Wordpress http://www.wptouch.com/; ModX http://modx.com/; TextPattern http://textpattern.com/; Refinery http://www.refinerycms.com/; Concrete5 http://www.concrete5.org/; Umbraco http://umbraco.com/; TinyCMS http://www.tinycms.eu/; GetSimpleCMS http://get-simple.info/; Pligg http://pligg.com/

Chapter 3 – Plug-ins and Services

If you you just want a blog; AnchorCMS, htmly, PivotX, Concrete5, Dropplets, Flatpress, Stacey, Textpress, or Serendipity[56] may offer you all you need at a lighter footprint. Most of these are complete CMS; that is they provide more than just a blog.

If you just need a blog, the easiest approach to keeping your website small may be to use Wordpress just for your blog, but not for other pages.

Wordpress allows you to copy certain articles from your Wordpress page to other PHP pages on your website.

Place this code directly after the `<body>` tag on that other page of your website:

```
<?PHP
require('../huggingthewind.yellowbearjourneys.com/
wp-blog-header.PHP');
?>
```

Place this code where you want the article to appear:

```
<?PHP
$my_postid = 82; //This is page id or post id,
change as needed
$title = get_the_title($my_postid);
echo "<br /><b>" . $title . "</b>";
$content_post = get_post($my_postid);
$content = $content_post->post_content;
$content = apply_filters('the_content', $content);
$content = str_replace(']]>', ']]&gt;', $content);
```

---

[55] vivalogo lightweight CMS list http://www.vivalogo.com/vl-resources/free-lightweight-simple-cms.htm

[56] AnchorCMS http://anchorcms.com/; htmly https://www.htmly.com/; PivotX http://pivotx.net/; Concrete5 http://www.concrete5.org/; Dropplets http://dropplets.com/; Flatpress http://flatpress.org/home/; Stacey http://www.staceyapp.com/; TextPress http://textpress.shameerc.com/; Serendipity http://www.s9y.org/

Designing your Website to Use Less Energy

```
   //echo apply_filters('the_content',
get_post_field('post_content', $post_id)); // remove
comment if you want to use the styling of your
Wordpress theme
   //remove last 2 div which contains share buttons -
the number of divs containing share buttons varies
depending on your share button plug-in
   $content =
substr($content,0,strripos($content,"<div")-1);
   $content =
substr($content,0,strripos($content,"<div")-1);
   echo $content;
   ?>
```

Chapter 3 – Plug-ins and Services

jQuery and Other Javascript Libraries (Frameworks)

If you're using a Javascript Library such as jQuery or MooTools, consider using a smaller Javascript Library (sometimes called Frameworks), many of which can be found at http://microjs.com/#.

Just place your cursor in the "I need ..." box and chose the selection you need. (You can alternatively type something in that box.) Also consider if you can write the code in straight Javascript (or PHP if on a PHP page).

If you still need jQuery, use the latest version as specified by jQuery.[57] jQuery comes in 2 major versions. Version 2 can be used so long as you're not worried about IE8 users. If you are, use version 1; but not that many people use IE8. The latest jQuery version as of this writing is 2.1.4.[58]

The main issue with using jQuery and other Javascript Libraries is the time it takes for them to load. With jQuery

---

[57] Latest jQuery version http://jquery.com/download/
[58] Version 2.1.4 – 2 is the major version, 1 is the minor version, 4 is the revision.

Designing your Website
to Use Less Energy

at least, the older the version, the slower it loads. The next issue with jQuery is, besides being a lot of code, you may be using plug-ins, which means even more code to load.

Make sure your plug-ins are upgraded to the latest version and check to make sure they're lightweight.

The top reasons for using jQuery are: DOM Manipulation; AJAX; Changes to the CSS; Animation; Effects; Managing Events; Looping; and Filtering results.

If you are using jQuery, only load it on the pages where you are using it.

Chapter 3 – Plug-ins and Services

CDN – Content Delivery Networks

jQuery (and many other Javascript libraries and other services) can be loaded to your website (if you have room), or they can be accessed from a CDN. CDN's ensure speedy loading. They ensure you have the latest upgrades, though at least with jQuery, they only ensure you have the latest upgrades for the version (2.1.4 or whatever) that you're accessing.

A CDN may load content faster than if it's loaded to your website. But, just using a CDN may not solve your page load speed issues.

jQuery has its own CDN[59]. jQuery can also be accessed from these CDNs – Google, Microsoft Ajax, CDNJS on Cloudflare, and jsDelivr.[60] It is probably fastest to load jQuery from its own CDN.

The following can be served from the Google CDN: Angular, Dojo, Ext Core, jQuery, Mootools, Prototype, script.aculo.us, SPF, SWFObject, three.js, and WebFontLoader.

---

[59] jQuery CDN http://jquery.com/download/
[60] Google CDN https://developers.google.com/speed/libraries/; Microsoft CDN http://www.asp.net/ajax/cdn; CDNJS https://cdnjs.com/; jsDelivr https://www.jsdelivr.com/

Designing your Website to Use Less Energy

The following can be served from the Microsoft CDN: jQuery, Ajax Control Toolkit, ASP.Net, Modernizer, JSHint, Knockout, Globalize, Respond, Bootstrap, Bootstrap TouchCarousel, and Hammer.js.

Several things can be served from CDNJS – too numerous to list. More than 1600 open source projects can be served by jsDelivr.

The library or font or … that you want served to your website will probably be served just as fast from any of these CDN, if the service is on multiple CDNs. The Speed considerations you may want to think about are

1) if multiple things are being served to your website, you may want to serve them all from the same CDN. Pulling them from the same CDN may be faster, or it may be faster to pull them from different CDNs. It probably makes no difference.

2) jsDelivr serves from whichever CDN is fastest for that user at that point in time for what you're requesting to be served, including jsDelivr's CDN (provided it's hosted on multiple CDNs).

If a library has its own CDN that may be the fastest, so long as their CDN is hosted on a fast CDN like MaxCDN.

An article on Lickity Split discusses the tradeoffs between serving a library from a CDN and serving it from your website.[61] The article favors serving from a CDN.

Scott Hanselman has an article on his blog discussing several ways to fall back from a CDN to your website for serving a library, in case the CDN is down.[62]

---

[61] Lickity Split CDN tradeoff article
https://zoompf.com/blog/2010/01/should-you-use-javascript-library-cdns
[62] Scott Hanselman article. Fallback from CDN
http://www.hanselman.com/blog/CDNsFailButYourScriptsDontHaveT

Chapter 3 – Plug-ins and Services

Another consideration for which CDN to use is that a library may have different bells and whistles on some CDNs than it has on others, depending on where developers have placed their plug-ins for that library.

Designing your Website to Use Less Energy

Make your Website Interactive

Interactive websites are those where you fill out a form and the response comes back on the same page, rather than transferring you to another page. These webpages are termed asynchronous. AJAX (Asynchronous Javascript with XML) is a common method of achieving this result. jQuery and other Javascript libraries are often used for AJAX.

Achieving better performance for these Javascript libraries is discussed in Chapter 2 – Performance Step 5 – Lighten your Javascript ***.

Chapter 3 – Plug-ins and Services

Forms Management

If you are using a Javascript Library or a CMS, there are probably plug-ins for Form Management. Choose a plug-in that's light-weight, but does what you need.

Alternately, you can write your own with PHP and HTML.

```
<form class="contact_form" name="contactform"
method="post" target="iframe_reply"
action="http://.../send_form_email.PHP">
  <b>Name</b><br /><input name="name" size="30"
/><br />
  <b>Email</b><br /><input name="email" size="30"
/><br />
  Sign me up for the newsletter<br /><br />
  <b>Comments</b><br />
  <textarea maxlength="500" placeholder="Additional
information" name="comments"></textarea><br />
  Help stop spam by entering these letters in
reverse order 
  <?PHP
  $xtra =
substr(str_shuffle("ABCDEFGHIJKLMNOPQRSTUVWXYZ"),0,3)
;
  print_r('<input size="1" type="text" name="xtra"
id="xtra" style="border:none; background-
color:#a0c0b0;" value="' . $xtra . '" readonly />')
  ?>
  <input type="text" name="botcheck" id="botcheck"
size="1" /><br />
```

```
  <input type="submit" value="Request it"
for="submit" />
  <label for="submit" id="submitmessage"></label><br
/><br />
  <iframe name="iframe_reply"
id="iframe_reply"></iframe><br />
  </form>
```

The form named `contactform` is filled in. When the user clicks the Submit, the action `send_form_email.PHP` is executed. `send_form_email.PHP` validates the form. At the end, it returns an error message or sends an email and returns a success message. The message is returned to the target which is an `iframe` within the form.

Using an iframe gets around having to use AJAX to return to the same page. The target could be another page, especially if there is more information to gather. You can also alter form fields in `send_form_email.PHP` to get around using an `iframe`.

Check out this AJAX example from W3Schools[63]. It uses PHP, but other uses of AJAX wouldn't need PHP. It also creates an HTTPRequest, and your Green Energy Website should keep those to a minimum.

```
send_form_email.PHP
<?
{
    // EDIT THE 2 LINES BELOW AS REQUIRED
    $email_to = "email@myemail.com";
    $email_subject = "Add me to the Mailing List";


    $name = $_POST['name']; // required
    $email_from = $_POST['email']; // required
    $comments = $_POST['comments'];
    $xtra = $_POST['xtra'];
    $botcheck = $_POST['botcheck'];
```

---

[63] W3Schools AJAX example
http://www.w3schools.com/PHP/PHP_ajax_PHP.asp

Chapter 3 – Plug-ins and Services

```
     $error_message = '<div
class="error_message">';
     $init_error_message_length =
strlen($error_message);

     if (!filter_var($name, FILTER_VALIDATE_REGEXP,
array('options' => array('regexp' => "/^[a-zA-Z0-9
.'-]+$/")))) {
          $error_message .= '*** The Name you entered
does not appear to be valid.<br />';
     }

     if (!filter_var($email_from,
FILTER_VALIDATE_EMAIL)) {
          $error_message .= '*** The Email Address
'.$email_from.' you entered does not appear to be
valid.<br />';
     }
     $botcheck = strtoupper($botcheck);
     $botcheck = str_replace(' ', '', $botcheck);
     if ( ! ( $botcheck == strrev($xtra) )) {
          $error_message .= '*** The anti-spam field
you entered does not appear to be valid.<br />';
     }

   if(strlen($error_message) ==
$init_error_message_length)
    {
       $email_message = "";

       function clean_string($string) {
          $bad = array("content-
type","bcc:","to:","cc:","href");
          return str_replace($bad,"",$string);
       }

       $email_message .= "Please sign me up for your
Mailing List\n";
       $email_message .= "".clean_string($name)."\n";
       $email_message .= "at
".clean_string($email_from)."\n";
       $email_message .=
clean_string($comments)."\n";
       //make sure each line is not more than 70
characters
       $email_message = wordwrap($email_message, 70);
```

Designing your Website to Use Less Energy

```php
$headers = "";
$headers .= 'From: '.$email_to."\r\n".
$headers .= "Reply-To: " . $email_to . "\r\n";
$headers .= "X-Mailer: PHP/" . phpversion();
mail($email_to, $email_subject, $email_message,
$headers, "-f$email_to");

    $error_message .= "Thank you for contacting
us. We will be in touch with you shortly.";
}
$error_message .= "</div>";
echo $error_message;
}
?>
```

Chapter 3 – Plug-ins and Services

Captchas

Captchas verify that the form is being filled out by a person rather than a bot. Captchas can be unfriendly and hard for humans to fill out, especially for the visually impaired.

Some captchas have an audio version. But that is often hard to understand.

Making the user do math or manipulate a string are more user-friendly, so long as they are not too difficult.

The captcha should incorporate randomness, so the same answer is not always entered for verification.

You may have noticed that the form code above uses an extra bit of PHP to create a Captcha. This Captcha asks the user to reverse the text and enter it to show they're a person rather than a bot.

Captchas also have a larger footprint than simple PHP code because they communicate with an external source. Perhaps it's not a much larger footprint. But it's still a footprint.

The top captcha is ReCaptcha[64] (Google Captcha) which observes the users behavior with the captcha to determine if

Designing your Website
to Use Less Energy

it's human or a bot. From the users viewpoint, the captcha consist of checking a checkbox to verify that you are human.

You may want to check out these lightweight captchas – Responsive-Captcha and Wheezy Captcha[65] (if you use python).

---

[64] Recaptcha https://www.google.com/recaptcha/intro/index.html
[65] Lightweight Captchas: Responsive-Captcha https://github.com/chrisvanpatten/responsive-recaptcha; Wheezy Captcha https://pypi.python.org/pypi/wheezy.captcha

Chapter 3 – Plug-ins and Services

Comments and Guestbook

Disqus, IntenseDebate, Gigya, and HTMLCommentBox[66] are popular comment plug-ins.

Disqus defaults to requiring users to log-in to Disqus before leaving a comment. Many popular websites use Disqus, so users who are used to leaving comments may already have a Disqus account.

IntenseDebate is similar to Disqus in many respects, but supposedly easier for users to use. For instance you can respond via email.

Gigya has a login. But users can login via a social network.

HTMLCommentBox has you log into your Google Account in order to be the moderator.

Facebook offers its own comment plug-in[67] which requires the user to be logged into Facebook. If a user uses Facebook, they are probably logged in, but contrary to Facebook's belief, not everybody is on Facebook.

You can use PHP to add Comments to your website. PHP comment scripts include Commentics and

---

[66] Comment plug-ins: Disqus https://disqus.com/; Gigya http://www.gigya.com/; HTMLCommentBox https://www.htmlcommentbox.com/

[67] Facebook Comment plug-in https://www.htmlcommentbox.com/

Designing your Website
to Use Less Energy

GentleSource[68]. You could use a form to create your own comment box. But it would only allow for one comment, unless you got fancy, in which case you might as well use a PHP script.

Comments need to be stored somewhere such as a database.

Although PHP scripts may be lighter weight than plug-ins, they may not offer you the security you want to prevent spamming.

Whatever option you employ, you should leave users an alternate method of leaving a comment, such as emailing you.

---

[68] PHP Comment scripts: Commentics https://www.commentics.org/; GentleSource http://www.gentlesource.com/comment-script/ (May require license.)

Chapter 3 – Plug-ins and Services

Social Sharing Buttons

AddThis, ShareThis, and AddtoAny[69] are popular plug-ins for sharing content on any website. Facebook[70], Twitter[71], and other social websites have their own buttons which you can add to your website.

These plug-ins and buttons can cause your website to load slowly. If you want to add buttons manually, follow the instructions from the social media platform or use the cheatsheet by Pamela Vaughan.[72]

Social9 is a very lightweight social sharing app which I now use. It has all the buttons you'll want or need.

AddThis, ShareThis, and AddtoAny offer buttons for practically every social platform, plus email.

---

[69] Popular Social Share Button plug-ins: AddThis http://www.addthis.com/; ShareThis http://www.sharethis.com/; AddtoAny https://www.addtoany.com/
[70] Facebook Like Button https://developers.facebook.com/docs/plugins/like-button
[71] Twitter Tweet Button https://about.twitter.com/resources/buttons#tweet
[72] Pamela Vaughan Social Media Button Cheatsheet http://blog.hubspot.com/blog/tabid/6307/bid/29544/The-Ultimate-Cheat-Sheet-for-Creating-Social-Media-Buttons.aspx

Designing your Website to Use Less Energy

AddThis offers a print button. The fewer buttons you show, the faster your website loads.

AddtoAny also offers a subscribe button for your RSS Feed (Blog).

The top social media apps are Facebook, Twitter, Pinterest, LinkedIn, and Tumblr. I would only include Pinterest if you're sharing pictures. I include an email button and a print button.

ATLChris tells how to create your own share buttons which carry a much lighter footprint than using any of the plug-ins[73]. The article is from 2010, so things may have changed. Check social-share-urls for up to date rules.[74] Share Link Generator will generate the links for you.[75]

To create a social sharing link, you basically pass the encoded URL and the Title to the social media app via a link `<a href=… />`.

ALTChris tells how to encode the URL with PHP and Wordpress. You can use the `encodeURIComponent` function in Javascript `x=encodeURIComponent(uri)`. Javascript refers to the URL as a URI – technically they're different, but for our purposes they're the same.

Facebook sharer link becomes `'https://www.facebook.com/sharer/sharer.PHP?u='+urlencoded`. All other parameters are picked up from the following `<meta>` tags in the `<head>` section of your webpage.

```
<meta property="og:title" content="My Webpage Title" />
<meta property="og:url" content="myurl">
```

---

[73] ATLChris DIY share buttons http://atlchris.com/1665/how-to-create-custom-share-buttons-for-all-the-popular-social-services/

[74] social-share-urls https://github.com/bradvin/social-share-urls

[75] Share Link Generator http://www.sharelinkgenerator.com/

Chapter 3 – Plug-ins and Services

```
<meta property="og:image" content="myimagesource"
/><!-- should not be generic; size 200x200-->
<meta property="og:description" content="My
website description." /><!--Should be at least 2
sentences -->
<meta property="og:site_name" content="My Website
Title" />
```

None of those link rules include a print button. To create a print button, use `window.print()`.

```
<a href="javascript:window.print()">Print</a>
```

Use this Javascript to obtain the information from your `og:` and `twitter:` `<meta>` tags.

```
var metas = document.getElementsByTagName('meta');
for (i = 0; i < metas.length; i++) {
    if (metas[i].getAttribute('property') ==
'og:title') {og_title =
encodeURIComponent(metas[i].getAttribute('content'));
}
    if (metas[i].getAttribute('property') ==
'og:url') {og_url =
encodeURIComponent(metas[i].getAttribute('content'));
}
    if (metas[i].getAttribute('property') ==
'og:image') {og_image =
encodeURIComponent(metas[i].getAttribute('content'));
}
    if (metas[i].getAttribute('property') ==
'og:description') {og_description =
encodeURIComponent(metas[i].getAttribute('content'));
}
    if (metas[i].getAttribute('property') ==
'og:site_name') {og_site_name =
encodeURIComponent(metas[i].getAttribute('content'));
}
    if (metas[i].getAttribute('name') ==
'twitter:card') {twitter_card =
encodeURIComponent(metas[i].getAttribute('content'));
}
    if (metas[i].getAttribute('name') ==
'twitter:site') {twitter_site =
encodeURIComponent(metas[i].getAttribute('content'));
}
```

Designing your Website
to Use Less Energy

```
        if (metas[i].getAttribute('name') ==
'twitter:title') {twitter_title =
encodeURIComponent(metas[i].getAttribute('content'));
}
        if (metas[i].getAttribute('name') ==
'twitter:description') {twitter_description =
encodeURIComponent(metas[i].getAttribute('content'));
}
        if (metas[i].getAttribute('name') ==
'twitter:image') {twitter_image =
encodeURIComponent(metas[i].getAttribute('content'));
}
    }
```

There are many sources for free social media buttons[76].

Contact me for programming services to help you set up your own Social Media Buttons (for a fee). I used Unicode characters (rather than images) on a background image to keep the buttons extra lightweight. But legally, you're supposed to use the images supplied by each Social Sharing Network. So, I switched to using those.

---

[76] Free Social Media Button images
http://www.vandelaydesign.com/free-social-media-icons/,
http://designscrazed.org/free-social-media-icons/, and
http://www.cssauthor.com/free-social-media-icon-sets/.

Chapter 3 – Plug-ins and Services

Maps and GPS

The most popular maps for websites are Google Maps and Bing Maps.[77] These use an iframe to display the map on your website. So they are lightweight.

There are specialty map sites like National Geographic.[78] Search for the specialty map you need.

Leaflet and Mapbox[79] let you build your own maps. Snazzy Maps[80] adds a color overlay onto Google Maps via Javascript and an event listener. The Javascript and event listener are lightweight.

To embed a map on your website with Google, click on the Menu button (three horizontal lines) and then click on the embed button and copy the code.
For Bing, click on the share button and copy the code. You may want to modify the code or remove pieces of the code.

---

[77] Google Maps https://www.google.com/maps; Bing Maps https://www.bing.com/maps/
[78] National Geographic Maps http://maps.nationalgeographic.com/maps
[79] Leaflet http://leafletjs.com/; Mapbox https://www.mapbox.com/
[80] Snazzy Maps https://snazzymaps.com/

Designing your Website
to Use Less Energy

HTML5 Geolocation[81] can be used to obtain a user's current coordinates, altitude, heading, and speed (with the user's permission).

FreeMapTools[82] offers various alternative maps like radius around a point, area calculators, population maps, and altitude.

If you need the latitude and longitude, grab them from the embed code from Google Maps or Bing Maps.

You can create your own embed data for any online map with an `iframe`. So long as you have a URL which points to that particular map.

---

[81] HTML5 Geolocation
http://www.w3schools.com/html/html5_geolocation.asp
[82] FreeMapTools http://www.freemaptools.com/

Chapter 3 – Plug-ins and Services

External Feeds including RSS

Managing the performance of external feeds has been discussed in Chapter 2 – Performance Step 2 – Limit External Feeds ***.

If you have a Wordpress Blog, you can copy articles to other places on your website with PHP. After `<body>` add

```
<?PHP
require('../blog-path-minus-http/wp-blog-
header.PHP');
?>
```

Where you want to include the article, add

```
<?PHP
$my_postid = 78;//This is page id or post id
$title = get_the_title($my_postid);
echo "<br /><b>" . $title . "</b>";
$content_post = get_post($my_postid);
$content = $content_post->post_content;
$content = apply_filters('the_content', $content);
$content = str_replace(']]>', ']]&gt;', $content);
//echo apply_filters('the_content',
get_post_field('post_content', $post_id));
//remove last 2 div which contains share buttons
$content =
substr($content,0,strripos($content,"<div")-1);
$content =
substr($content,0,strripos($content,"<div")-1);
```

Designing your Website
to Use Less Energy

```
echo $content;
?>
```

The number of divs you remove for share buttons will depend on the share plug-in.

You can embed RSS feeds on your website with Feed Wind, RSS2HTML, and Surfing Waves[83]. Each of these services use a Javascript library to display the RSS feed. There are RSS feed plug-ins for jQuery.

A simpler method may be to use oEmbed[84]. A simpler version of oEmbed can be found at embed.ly[85]. embed.ly uses oEmbed to return RSS, Twitter, Facebook, and other feeds. Speed depends on the embed.ly Javascript library (very small) and the oEmbed technology which is incorporated into feed sites and feed CMS (lightweight).

---

[83] Embed RSS Feeds with Feed Wind http://feed.mikle.com/; RSS2HTML http://rss.bloople.net/; Surfing Waves http://www.surfing-waves.com/feed.htm

[84] oEmbed http://oembed.com/

[85] embed.ly http://embed.ly/

Chapter 3 – Plug-ins and Services

Photo Gallery and Image Management

There are several slideshow and photo gallery scripts. PHPSlideShow[86] is a popular one for slide shows. Popular plug-ins for Photo Galleries are Piwigo, Coppermine, ZenPhoto, and TinyWebGallery[87]. Of these, TinyWebGallery has the smallest install file. The others are much larger.

For an even smaller footprint consider phpAlbum (very small), PixelPost, and Plogger.[88]

PictureFill[89] may be useful for displaying images at various sizes and resolutions depending on various conditions, such as screen size.

---

[86] PHPSlideshow http://www.zinkwazi.com/scripts/

[87] Popular Photo Gallery plug-ins: Piwigo http://piwigo.org/; Coppermine http://coppermine-gallery.net/; ZenPhoto http://www.zenphoto.org/; TinyWebGallery http://www.tinywebgallery.com/

[88] Lightweight Photo Gallery plug-ins: phpAlbum http://phpalbum.net/; PixelPost http://www.pixelpost.org/; Plogger http://www.plogger.org/

[89] PictureFill http://scottjehl.github.io/picturefill/

Designing your Website to Use Less Energy

Webstores, Shopping Carts, and Buy Buttons

For ecommerce, you'll want to look at security more than at energy savings.

Your webhost may offer a webstore or rather membership in a partner's webstore. These will have lots of traffic. So they should be well maintained and load quickly.

They will probably also have better security than a webstore you set up on your own.

CafeCommerceSA, PrestaShop, BigCommerce, Shopify, Miva, DemandWare, 3D Cart, and Yahoo Small Business Ecommerce are popular webstores.[90]

Your webhost may offer its own solution.

Etsy[91] is popular for selling crafts.

---

[90] Popular Webstores: CafeCommerceSA http://www.cafecommercesa.org/; PrestaShop https://www.prestashop.com/; BigCommerce https://www.bigcommerce.com/; Shopify https://www.shopify.com/; Miva http://www.miva.com/; DemandWare http://www.demandware.com/; 3DCart http://www.3dcart.com/; Yahoo Small Business https://smallbusiness.yahoo.com/ecommerce

[91] Etsy https://www.etsy.com/

Chapter 3 – Plug-ins and Services

OpenCart, Volusion, and Demandware[92] are popular ecommerce CMS.

ZenCart[93] is a popular shopping cart.

Other selling options include PayPal, Stripe, Selz, Navigate Starter, Dwolla, 2Checkout, Gumroad, and Sellfy[94].

Selz has a small footprint, an online store, and buy buttons which can be placed on your website or in an email. However, it can take some work to keep your webpages mobile-friendly.

Contact me if you need consulting help.

---

[92] Popular Ecommerce CSM: OpenCart http://www.opencart.com/; Volusion http://www.volusion.com/; DemandWare http://www.demandware.com/

[93] Zen-Cart https://www.zen-cart.com/

[94] Other selling options: PayPal https://www.paypal.com/home; Stripe https://stripe.com/; Selz https://selz.com/; Navigate Starter http://payment-gateways.credio.com/l/77/NaviGate-Starter; Dwolla https://www.dwolla.com/; 2Checkout https://www.2checkout.com/; Gumroad https://gumroad.com/; Sellfy https://sellfy.com/

Designing your Website
to Use Less Energy

Chat

Pure Chat, tawk.to, olark, mylivechat, and Zopim are popular Chat plug-ins.[95] No word on whether they're light weight or not, so you'll need to test those that have free trials or are free and see which one loads quickest.

Before installing a Chat add-in, consider if it will help you. Will you be available to chat or can you hire operators to chat for you? If you hire operators, how much of your time will be taken training them?

Some Chat add-ins do allow you to reply with canned responses. Do you have canned responses or static answers? Do you want a more personalized approach? And, how many possible sales are you really missing.

---

[95] Popular Chat plug-ins: Pure Chat
https://www.purechat.com/home; tawk.to https://www.tawk.to/; olark https://www.olark.com/; mylivechat https://mylivechat.com/; Zopim https://www.zopim.com/

Chapter 3 – Plug-ins and Services

Search

Search includes searching your website and providing a custom search for your users. Google, Bing, and other search engines offer Custom Search APIs.

If you want a lighter-weight option for searching your website, consider creating a user-friendly sitemap as a separate page to your website. You may want to title the sitemap as Website Index or Search this Website. The sitemap would simply contain links to your other pages.

XML-Sitemaps and Sitemap X[96] generate HTML sitemaps for your website. They also generate an XML sitemap for search engines.

If you want a lighter-weight option for a custom search, consider doing the search yourself and adding links of those results to your search engine. This allows you to manually filter the results.

On the other hand, you'll need to fix broken links and make sure the links still link to what you think they do, from time to time.

---

[96] XML-Sitemaps https://www.xml-sitemaps.com/; Sitemap X http://www.sitemapx.com/

Designing your Website
to Use Less Energy

You can use an `iframe` which references a search URL from Google, Bing, etc.

Adding `site:http://yoursite.com` to a Google Search will cause the search to search your website.

Chapter 3 – Plug-ins and Services

Event Calendars for Appointments and Scheduling

Places of Lodging, Restaurants with bookable space, and others may need to have an Event Calendar on the website for appointments and scheduling. You may want to post a calendar of your business's events on your website.

If you just have a few events, manually create a box (perhaps a `div` with a border) in HTML to show these events.

If you need a more robust calendar, consider Webcalendar.[97] It uses PHP and MySQL and is lightweight.
Google Calendar and iCal (if you have a Mac) are popular website calendar add-ins.

An article on app storm lists 15 Calendar plug-ins.[98]

----

[97] WebCalendar http://www.k5n.us/webcalendar.php
[98] app storm Calendar plug-ins article
http://web.appstorm.net/roundups/15-cool-alternatives-to-google-calendar/

Designing your Website
to Use Less Energy

Communities and Restricted Access (Members Only)

Most CMS offer plug-ins to build a Community where members can interact with each other. Spruz and Wall.FM let you build your own Community or Social Network.

Most social networks allow you to create groups.

Consider if you really need a community, what advantages there will be for those who join your community, and if/how you will monitor discussions and requests to join before creating your own community.

It may be best to create a group on a social network first. When it becomes popular, you can alert members to a community you'll host elsewhere so members don't have to be on a particular social network to have access to your group.

Also consider if members are really having discussions or if they are just posting links to their blogs. Either or both may be fine, depending on what you want.

Chapter 3 – Plug-ins and Services

Video and Audio

The simplest way to embed video or audio on your website is to first create the video or audio – using your webcam, smartphone, digital camera, or a more sophisticated and professional looking method like YouTube Capture.[99]

Then upload the video / audio to a popular video website: YouTube, Vimeo, Vevo (mostly for music), Veoh, Flickr, and Break (for funny videos).[100]

Then grab the embed code and place it on your website.

Allow the user to start audio and video rather than autostarting them. Links to Youtube videos include `/watch`. Remove the `/watch` to have the video not autostart.

Options for just placing the video on your website include Flowplayer, Cincopa, Video.JS.[101] Sound Clouds was recommended by Audible Books.

---

[99] YouTube Capture https://www.youtube.com/capture

[100] YouTube https://www.youtube.com/; Vimeo https://vimeo.com/; Vevo http://www.vevo.com/; Veoh http://www.veoh.com/; Flickr https://www.flickr.com/ ; Break http://www.break.com/

[101] Flowplayer https://flowplayer.org/; Cincopa http://www.cincopa.com/; Video.JS http://videojs.com/

Designing your Website to Use Less Energy

Most other options are Flash based and should not be used since Flash is losing support from browsers, is usually slow, and has security risks.

Video.JS uses the HTML5 `<video>` tag and CSS, which is probably the lightest footprint. If the footprint is still larger than you want, consider writing your own using the HTML5 `<video>` tag and CSS.[102]

Remember to not specify `autoplay`. That way, users can start the video when they want to and your website will save energy.

Specify `control` so that users can control the video, especially if you do not specify `autoplay`. You'll probably want to specify `preload="metadata"` which preloads tracklist, length, and first frame. If you specify `autoplay`, `preload` will be ignored.

Browsers may load less than you specify. That generally improves the users experience.

The HTML5 `<audio>` tag works similarly.[103]

Also refer to the Photo Gallery Management section to create photo and slide shows. Other tools include PowerPoint, kizoa, smilebox, photosnack, Slidely, and ROXIO Photoshow.[104]

No matter which method you use, you probably will want to upload your video / audio to the popular video websites listed above.

---

[102] `<video>` tag http://www.w3schools.com/tags/tag_video.asp

[103] `<audio>` tag http://www.w3schools.com/tags/tag_audio.asp

[104] PowerPoint (part of Microsoft Office https://products.office.com/en-US/) ; kizoa http://www.kizoa.com/; smilebox http://www.smilebox.com/; photosnack http://www.photosnack.com/; Slidely http://slide.ly/; ROXIO Photoshow http://www.photoshow.com/

Chapter 3 – Plug-ins and Services

The higher the resolution of the video and audio, the more energy it will take to play it. On the other hand, you don't want the resolution to be too low.

Youtube, Vimeo, and others give their recommendations for the best resolutions. Standard Definition should work well with a 16:9 ration (640 x 360 px) for images. AAC-LC Codec (LC for Low-Complexity), Data Rate of 320 kbits/sec, and Sample Rate of 48 kHz are recommended.

No doubt YouTube Capture will choose the best rate. They want the video to look well, but not take too much energy, since they're paying for that energy.

Remember videos do not have to include audio.

If you want to record an interview or call with another person for your website, get that person's permission first. You can use a Skype plug-in or possibly your Smartphone to do this.

Designing your Website
to Use Less Energy

Animation

Animation consists of changing the x, y coordinates every so often over time. You could also animate other aspects of the drawing such as width, height, color, text, and shape. You can also change the entire drawing or image.

jQuery, Swipe, Shifty, Morpheus, Morf, and Viper[105] are Javascript libraries which help with Animation or Tweening.

jQuery has a large footprint, the others have small footprints.

Alternatively, you can write your own animations using Javascript and CSS3 Transitions as Morf does. Or you can just use CSS3 Transitions (and CSS3 Transforms).[106]

---

[105] jQuery https://jquery.com/; Swipe https://github.com/thebird/swipe; Shifty https://github.com/jeremyckahn/shifty; Morpheus https://github.com/ded/morpheus; Morf https://github.com/joelambert/morf; Viper https://github.com/alpha123/Viper

[106] CSS3 Transitions http://www.w3schools.com/CSS/css3_transitions.asp; CSS3 Transforms http://www.w3schools.com/cssref/css3_pr_transform.asp

Chapter 3 – Plug-ins and Services

CSS3 will be the lightest footprint. Javascript plus CSS3 will be the next lightest footprint.

You can also use Javascript plus HTML5 Canvas for a lightweight animation.

Designing your Website to Use Less Energy

Weather

The Weather Channel, Weather Underground, AccuWeather, NOAA, Forecast, WeatherSpark, Intellicast, Google Weather, CNN Weather, and WeatherBug are popular weather websites.[107] Most of these have embed code for your website. Some of them require you to use their API.

For Google Weather, just go to Google Search, and type Weather followed by a location. You may want to use the Google Search API to create a custom search using Google Weather and just return the first result to your Website. See Search.

If you want a weather website showing you how to dress for the weather, try Daily Dress Me, Dress Caillou, Obama Weather (featuring Barack Obama, Bruce Lee, and

---

[107] The Weather Channel http://www.weather.com/; Weather Underground http://www.wunderground.com/; AccuWeather http://www.accuweather.com/; NOAA http://www.noaa.gov/; Forecast http://forecast.io/; WeatherSpark https://weatherspark.com/; Intellicast http://www.intellicast.com/; Google Weather https://www.google.com/search?q=google+weather; CNN Weather http://www.cnn.com/weather; WeatherBug http://weather.weatherbug.com/

Chapter 3 – Plug-ins and Services

Angelina Jolie), and KIM.GURU (featuring Kim Kardashian).[108]

weatherbase[109] gives the forecast, monthly averages, and a Climate Summary.

NOAA, Saltwater Tides, Tides.net, Wolfram Alpha, Twiddy Tide Charts, US Harbors, and FreeTideTables are popular Tide websites.[110] Some of these offer widgets for your website.

Tides.net stores daily tide images on their site. You can display these on your website by generating the image URL which follows the format

`http://www.tides.net/graph/site/yyyy/mm/dd_size.png.`

`site` is the tide site – just find the tide on their site to find out this number.

`yyyy/mm/dd` is the date.

`size` is `sm` for small or `lg` for large.

If you want to display water temperature on your website, look for a Water Temperature website – these are usually fishing websites.

Temperature Sea[111] offers a widget, but only for coastal waters. Water Quality for swimming at beaches can be found on NRDC and EPA websites.[112]

---

[108] Daily Dress Me http://dailydressme.com/; Dress Caillou http://pbskids.org/caillou/games/dresscaillou.html; Obama Weather http://obama-weather.com/; KIM.GURU http://kim.guru/

[109] weatherbase http://www.weatherbase.com/

[110] NOAA Tides https://tidesandcurrents.noaa.gov/tide_predictions.html; Saltwater Tides http://www.saltwatertides.com/; Tides.net http://www.tides.net/; Wolfram Alpha Tides http://www.wolframalpha.com/input/?i=tides; Twiddy Tide Charts https://www.twiddy.com/tide-charts/; US Harbors http://usharbors.com/; FreeTideTables http://www.freetidetables.com/

Designing your Website to Use Less Energy

Stormsurf and Surf-Forecast[113] display surfing conditions.

Many general weather websites along with On The Snow, Snow-Forecast, OpenSnow, SnowForecast, and SnoCountry[114] show Snow and Ski Forecasts.

NOAA, ORCAA, AirNow[115] display Air Quality Forecasts along with some other general weather websites.

General weather websites along with Pollen.com, American Academy of Allergy Asthma and Immunology (AAAAI), and Zyrtec[116] provide Pollen Forecasts.

Aviation Weather Center[117] displays – you guessed it – Flying Weather. Some general weather sites also display Aviation Weather.

The lightest weight weather implementation for your website will be to use code from NOAA, since most of the

---

[111] Temperature Sea http://seatemperature.info/

[112] Water Quality NRDC http://www.nrdc.org/water/oceans/ttw/; EPA http://www2.epa.gov/beaches/find-information-about-your-beach.

[113] Stormsurf http://www.stormsurf.com/; Surf-Forecast http://www.surf-forecast.com/

[114] On The Snow http://www.onthesnow.com/; Snow-Forecast http://www.snow-forecast.com/; OpenSnow https://opensnow.com/; SnowForecast http://www.snowforecast.com/; SnoCountry http://www.snocountry.com/

[115] NOAA Air Quality http://www.nws.noaa.gov/airquality/ww.shtml; ORCAA https://www.orcaa.org/; AirNow http://www.airnow.gov/

[116] Pollen.com http://www.pollen.com/allergy-weather-forecast.asp; AAAAI http://www.aaaai.org/global/nab-pollen-counts.aspx; Zyrtec https://www.zyrtec.com/allergy-forecast-tools-apps

[117] Aviation Weather Center https://www.aviationweather.gov/

Chapter 3 – Plug-ins and Services

other websites use that information for their weather – though they may alter it some before displaying it.

Create an `<iframe>` with `target=` `"http://forecast.weather.gov/zipcity.PHP?inputstring=` `city,%20st"`. Replace city with your city and st with your state abbreviation.

NOAA provides a REST API[118].

If you don't want to write your own script to handle the REST API, try the one at Saratoga-Weather[119] (not just weather for Saragota).

Or use the information from Vassar which uses PHP, HTML, and jQuery.[120] Vassar uses jQuery to update the weather every 15 minutes. So you can omit it if that update is not important.

Omitting the jQuery will make this a lightweight solution.

If you do want the update consider using a lightweight jQuery alternative listed on microjs.[121]

---

[118] NOAA Rest API
http://www.nws.noaa.gov/mdl/survey/pgb_survey/dev/rest.php
[119] Saratoga-Weather script http://saratoga-weather.org/scripts-carterlake.php
[120] Vassar weather script info
http://webdesign.vassar.edu/2012/07/dynamic-weather-with-noaa-PHP-jquery-and-html-templates/
[121] microjs http://microjs.com/#

Designing your Website to Use Less Energy

Financial Info including Stocks

If you're looking for Financial Information to display on your website, look at CNN Money, Kiplinger, This is Money, TheStreet, Seeking Alphaα, Bloomberg Business, Forbes, Investor Words, Market Watch, The Motley Fool, and Wise Bread.[122]

You may find add-ins on those sites. It's more likely that you'd use them as RSS Feeds.

Financial add-ins are available from Investing.com and theFinancials.[123]

---

[122] CNN Money http://money.cnn.com/; Kiplinger http://www.kiplinger.com/; This is Money http://www.thisismoney.co.uk/; TheStreet http://www.thestreet.com/; Seeking Alphaα http://seekingalpha.com/; Bloomburg Business http://www.bloomberg.com/; Forbes http://www.forbes.com/; Investor Words http://www.investorwords.com/; Market Watch http://www.marketwatch.com/; The Motley Fool http://www.fool.com/; Wise Bread http://www.wisebread.com/

[123] Investing.com http://www.investing.com/; theFinancials http://www.thefinancials.com/

Chapter 3 – Plug-ins and Services

For Stock widgets, look at TradingView, Free Stockcharts, StockCharts.com, FinancialContent.com, and AppuOnline.[124]

Coupon widgets can be found on LocalSaver and BeFrugal.[125]

If you want to create your own website coupons you can try Coupontank and Coupons in Demand.[126]
It will be easier and cheaper to just create an image for your coupon. Provide a link to the image, and let the user print that page. Not elegant, but it works.

You can also use the onclick event and Javascript to change all divs to hidden except the coupon div, print using `Windows.print`
And then change all the divs back to their original state (visible, hidden, etc).

Currency Converter add-ins can be found at xe, TransferMate, OANDA, USFOREX, and Exchange Rate.[127]

---

[124] TradingView https://www.tradingview.com/; Free Stockcharts http://www.freestockcharts.com/; StockCharts.com http://stockcharts.com/; FinancialContent.com http://www.financialcontent.com/free-stock-market-widgets/market-snapshot.PHP; AppuOnline http://www.appuonline.com/gadgets.html
[125] LocalSaver https://my.datasphere.com/sites/all/modules/custom/loosejaw_couponflow/wdgt/index.html; BeFrugal http://www.befrugal.com/tools/coupon-widget/
[126] Coupontank http://www.coupontank.com/; Coupons in Demand http://www.couponsindemand.com/
[127] xe http://www.xe.com/currencyconverter/customize.php; TransferMate https://www.transfermate.com/en/free_currency_converter.asp; OANDA http://www.oanda.com/currency/converter/; USFOREX

Designing your Website
to Use Less Energy

Translation

Google, Bing, and others provide Translation add-ins for websites. However, Chrome and Internet Explorer offer automatic page translation so you may not need to provide this service.

There are add-ons or extensions for the other browsers which offer translation services. (IE Edge will not have add-ons until 2016.)

Usually those who are reading websites which are not in their language have an automatic method of translating that website.

So there is little need to provide an add-in to your website.

The lightest weight method of providing your website in various languages would be to provide various versions, each in a different language.

The languages with the most native speakers are Mandarin, Spanish, English, Hindi, Arabic, Portuguese, Bengali, Russian, and Japanese.

---

http://www.usforex.com/about-us/partners-affiliates/partners-website-tools; Exchange Rate https://www.exchangeratewidget.com/currency-converter-widget/

Chapter 3 – Plug-ins and Services

Although 40% of the world only speaks one language, most of those people speak English. 43% of the world is bilingual. That second language is usually English, or French in some African locations.

13% of the world is trilingual with one of those languages often being English.

The remaining 4% speak more than three languages, one of which is often English.

If you decide to translate your website into multiple languages you might want to start with English and Mandarin since most of the world speaks one of those two languages. But you may want to start with a language that your website is targeted to.

If you do offer multiple language versions of your website, you'll want a menu the user can choose from.

You'll also want to detect their language. This can be done in Javascript with `navigator.userLanguage||navigator.language`. Use `navigator.browserLanguage` for IE10.

In PHP use `$_SERVER['HTTP_ACCEPT_LANGUAGE']` which returns an array of all the languages a user's browser can read.

You can set the language of your website content. If a webpage only contains on language, English for example, specify `<html lang="en">` or `<meta http-equiv="content-language" content="en">`. If it contains multiple languages use a comma delimited list. You can specify a specific language on an element of your website.

Designing your Website
to Use Less Energy

You can also specify the language of the entire website in `.htaccess` with `DefaultLanguage en-US`.

If you're trying to determine the language of a website, you may need to detect the location for those websites which do not specify the language – see Maps and GPS.

You can redirect you webpage based on the user's language. For instance, if you have a Mandarin version of the webpage, add this to the English version of your webpage (assuming the primary language is English). `<link rel="alternate" hreflang="zh" href="mandarin-webpage-url" />`.

To change styles or fonts based on language, use CSS Classes or CSS `:lang(en)` where `en` is the language code. You may also want to alter the width or font-size depending on the language.

For right-to-left languages (mainly Arabic and Hebrew) specify `<html dir="rtl">`.

You can find lists of language codes at W3Schools and at IANA (more specific).[128] IANA lists acceptable language codes in the form `language-subtag` or `language-region`. For example `en-US` for US English (US being a region) or `zh-cmn` for Mandarin.

`zh-gouyu` is an old standard for Mandarin which is still accepted. You can also specify `zh-cmn-Hans` for simplified Mandarin or `zh-cmn-Hant` for Traditional Mandarin.

---

[128] Language Code Lists W3Schools
http://www.w3schools.com/tags/ref_language_codes.asp; IANA
http://www.iana.org/assignments/language-subtag-registry/language-subtag-registry

Chapter 3 – Plug-ins and Services

Browsers may try to determine the language of the page from the content of the page, especially when no language is specified.

Not specifying a website language makes it difficult for screen readers which are often used by the visually impaired, to correctly read the website. It also makes it difficult for scripts trying to interpret the language.

Designing your Website
to Use Less Energy

Special Fonts

If you want to use or embed a special font on your website, one that's not a websafe font, use Google Fonts.[129]

If I want to use *Dancing Script* font from Google Fonts, I can add this to my stylesheet:

```
@import
url(http://fonts.googleapis.com/CSS?family=Dancing+Sc
ript);
```

Or I can add this to my html, which loads the font a little faster:

```
<link
href='http://fonts.googleapis.com/CSS?family=Dancing+
Script' rel='stylesheet' type='text/CSS'>
```

If I am just going to use this font for the phrase *Yellow Bear Journeys*, I can include just those characters as follows:

```
@import
url(http://fonts.googleapis.com/CSS?family=Dancing+Sc
ript&text=
Yellow%20Bear%20Journeys);
```

This will speed up loading of the font.

---

[129] Websafe fonts http://www.cssfontstack.com/; Google Fonts https://www.google.com/fonts

Chapter 3 – Plug-ins and Services

I suggest you just load the entire font. It won't take that long, especially not if you have modPageSpeed enabled. Just don't load too many fonts. Sooner or later you'll want more characters in your phrase or you'll want the normal version of the font.

Google Fonts makes the coding simple:
1) Find the font you want to use. Click "Add to Collection". Find the next font, click "Add to Collection". Etc.
2) At the bottom of the page (at Collection) on the right-hand side, click on "Use".
3) On the next page, check all the styles you want to use, check all the character sets you want to use, Click on "Standard" or "@import" and copy the code to your website ("Standard") or stylesheet ("@import").

Add the fonts to your font lists: `font-family: "Dancing Script", "Lucida Handwriting","Monotype Corsiva","Bradley Hand ITC","Brush Script MT", Arial, Helvetica, cursive;` Note: at this point, I can remove some of these other fonts from the list. I keep them there, since there may be a gap between Dancing Script being loaded and my page displaying.

The browser will use the next available font in my font-list until the font is loaded. This is not likely to ever happen. This is just a fail-safe.

You can now download Google Fonts directly from the Google Fonts website. You can also use SkyFonts[130] to download the fonts. SkyFonts also enables the download of

---

[130] SkyFonts https://skyfonts.com/

Designing your Website
to Use Less Energy

fonts from other font libraries (Fonts.com, MyFonts, Monotype, and Linotype[131]).

Google Fonts are free, the others may not be.

Just download Skyfonts, following the instructions.

Skyfonts constantly monitors the web for upgrades to your fonts. If you don't want it to do so, right-click on the SkyFonts icon in your system tray and choose settings. Uncheck, Start Skyfonts on Machine Startup. Then right-click the icon again and choose Quit Skyfonts.

If you want to use Brick Fonts, go to http://brick.im/fonts/ and click on the GITHUB link.

Adobe provides fonts at https://edgewebfonts.adobe.com/fonts and at https://typekit.com/fonts. (Typekit is not free.)

Go to EdgeWeb, Click on a font and choose "Select this font". Follow the instructions. These instructions only offer a Javascript option (e.g. (`abel` is the font name `<script src="//use.edgefonts.net/abel.js"></script>`) rather than `@import` or `link` option as with Google Fonts (though Google Fonts also offers a Javascript option).

Remember when testing fonts, that if a font exists on your computer, the browser will use it, unless you've told it how to find it on your website.

Try testing with an alternate name in `@font-face` for the font-family. For Google Fonts, try testing with a font you haven't downloaded to your computer.

```
@font-face {
    font-family: "Symbola";
```

---

[131] Fonts.com http://www.fonts.com/; MyFonts https://www.myfonts.com/; Monotype http://www.monotype.com/; Linotype http://www.linotype.com/

Chapter 3 – Plug-ins and Services

```
    src: local('Symbola'), url(Symbola.ttf);
}
```

Use `local` option first. This will make your page load faster if the user has that font installed on their computer.

Some applications like Font-Squirrel may help you use a subset of your font. However, if you're just using a few characters from a font, browsers should just load those characters and not the entire font.

Designing your Website
to Use Less Energy

Other Plug-Ins

Other plug-ins for websites include e-cards, calculators, and time-related plug-ins such as reminders.

If you need another plug-in search these sites POWr, i3dTHEMES, WolframAlpha, WidgetsCode, and 100widgets[132], or try writing your own[133].

---

[132] POWr https://www.powr.io/plugins; i3dTHEMES http://www.i3dthemes.com/; WolframAlpha http://www.wolframalpha.com/; WidgetsCode http://widgetscode.com/; 100widgets http://100widgets.com/

[133] Write your own plug-in Chapter 4 – Make your own Plug-in

Chapter 4 – Make your own Plug-in

What is involved in making your own plug-in?

That depends on what you want your plug-in to do and if you're writing it for HTML or for a CMS or Javascript Library?

- Will it manipulate information or images?

- Will it pull information from another website?

- Will it need to store data or query data?

- Will it need to run code from another site?

- Will it need to interact with the user?

Those are the basic questions.

Designing your Website to Use Less Energy

Manipulating Information or Images

Manipulating information can be done with Javascript or PHP for lightweight add-ins. Sometimes it can be transformed just by using CSS.

Images can be manipulated with HTML5 Canvas and Javascript for lightweight add-ins.

More extensive manipulation may need a lightweight Javascript Library. See Chapter 2 – Performance Step 5 – Lighten your Javascript ***.

Chapter 4 – Make your own Plug-in

Pulling Info from Another Website

Try to limit the number of other websites you're pulling information from.

Consider if you're pulling raw data and then making it user-friendly, or if you're pulling data that's already spruced up.

If there's an option, will the code you write be more light-weight than the code that's running on the other website?

Is the external source interacting with you in more ways than just offering you data?

Is the external source always up?

Will you provide a fall back for times when it's not up?

If you're just pulling in information already displayed on another website, you can try to use an `<iframe>`, though you'll want to limit the number of `<iframe>` tags on your site to make it load faster.

Videos should use <video> and audios should use <audio>. See Chapter 3 Plug-ins and Other Services Video and Audio for more information.

Designing your Website to Use Less Energy

cURL[134] is often used with PHP for pulling data from other websites.

You can also use the native PHP functions `file()`, `file_get_contents()`, and `readfile()`.[135]

jQuery can also be used.

---

[134] cURL http://curl.haxx.se/

[135] Pulling information from another website with `file()` and `file_get_contents()` http://cullenwebservices.com/how-to-pull-information-from-another-website/

Dale Stubbart   Page 107 of 135
Stubbart.com

Chapter 4 – Make your own Plug-in

Storing/Querying Data

If is usually faster to store data in a database on your website, rather than a database on another website. So, that is usually the better choice, unless there are security concerns (usually those are minimal).

MySQL is often the database which is offered by webhosts and may be your only choice. PHP is normally the language you'd interact with the database in, though you might use Ruby on Rails. See Chapter 2 Performance Step 9 – Check your Database Queries *** for more information.

The lightest weight method of storing and querying data may not be a database.

If the information is static (or only changes infrequently and you're the one changing it), consider an HTML list, which you access with Javascript. You can hide the list if you don't need it displayed.

If you need to maintain the information for the length of the user's visit to your website and you need to maintain it from page to page consider cookies.

If it's really simple, consider passing variables added onto the URL you're linking to and parsing them with PHP.

Designing your Website
to Use Less Energy

If the security of the variables matters, find another method.

Create your link as `<a href="contact.PHP?reasona">Contact Us for Reason A</a>` if you want to pass one piece of information or `<a href="contact.PHP?reasona='reasona'&reason='reasonb'& reasonc='reasonc'">Contact Us for Reason A</a>` if you want to pass multiple pieces of information. Of course you can combine all your information into the first information and parse it later if you want.

On your linked-to page, parse the information with `<?PHP print_r(ucfirst($_SERVER['QUERY_STRING'])) ?>` if you're just passing one piece of information.

If you're passing multiple pieces of information you can parse it with:

```
<?PHP
parse_str(parse_url ($url, PHP_URL_QUERY),$result)
reasona=$result['reasona']
reasonb=$result['reasonb']
reasonc=$result['reasonc']
?>
```

If you want to use the value on a form and you're just passing one parameter you can use:

```
<a href="contact.PHP?reasona">Contact Us for
Reason A</a>
```

and

```
<input type="checkbox" name="reasona" id="reasona"
value="Reason A" />
```

with this code before `</body>`

```
<script>
document.getElementById("reasona").checked =
false;
if ( location.search == "?reasona" ) {
    document.getElementById("reasona").checked =
true;
}
</script>
```

Chapter 4 – Make your own Plug-in

You can create / store data in a cookie which is stored on the user's computer. To create or change a cookie, use the following Javascript statement.

Pass the cookie expiration date in yyyy, mm, dd, hr (using 24 hour clock), mn, sc (seconds) to Date.UTC.

```
myDate=Date(Date.UTC(yyyy, mm, dd, hr, min, sec));
document.cookie="cookie1=Reason A;
expires='+myDate.toUTCString+'";
```

To read a cookie use var x = document.cookie;

To delete a cookie, change it to expire sometime in the past.

You can use PHP to read / write files stored with your website. You may want to format your files with XML for easier parsing.

The simplest method of reading data from a file with PHP is `<?PHP myfile=readfile("webdictionary.txt"); ?>`

To write or read data, use fopen, fread, fwrite, and fclose as follows.

w+ means read / write and when you write you're going to replace the entire file. Hopefully your file is small and rewriting the entire file will not take longer than adding data to the end or beginning of the file. You cannot replace only certain lines.

```
<?PHP
$myfile = fopen("myfile.txt", "w+");
$txt = fread($myfile,filesize("myfile.txt"));
//read entire file
// make changes to $txt
fwrite($myfile, $txt);
fclose($myfile);
?>
```

Designing your Website to Use Less Energy

Cookies can be used to store data for a user on their computer. However, if they browse your website from a different device, their data is not available.

Cookies should be limited as they can slow down your website.

Cookies need to be kept small (4000bytes/domain) and few (50/domain).

You'll also want to limit what you store in cookies for security reasons.

Cookies can be blocked by the user.

There are US Guidelines and European Guidelines you need to abide by for cookies, because they are stored on a user's computer.

Cookies are fine for storing small bits of non-identifying data. But there are better, faster methods like HTML5 Local Storage.[136]

---

[136] HTML5 Local Storage
http://www.w3schools.com/html/html5_webstorage.asp

Chapter 4 – Make your own Plug-in

Running Code from Another Site

If you need to run code from another site, it is usually loaded with `<link>` and that website will tell you how to use it.

Refer to Chapter 2 – Performance Step 2 – Limit External Feeds ***, to make it more lightweight. Also search to see if there is a more lightweight version which will work as well and as easily.

Designing your Website to Use Less Energy

Interacting with the User

Probably you will use a form to interact with the user, though there are other methods.

Refer to Chapter 3 – Plug-ins and Other Services Forms Management.

Chapter 5 – Choosing Colors

Dark colors take more energy to display than light colors unless you've got a really, really old screen (from 2005 or before) in which case light colors take more energy.

Avoiding dark colors helps your Green Energy Website save energy, even if only a little bit.

Instead of black, use `#101010` (avoid `0x` for red, green, and blue. You may also want to consider `DarkSlateGray`, `DarkSlateBlue`, `Navy`, `Maroon`, and `Olive`.

Google uses `#545454` for black text on a white background. Google changes the color they use for black text from time to time. It used to be `#343434`.

White backgrounds can cause eye strain. So you may want to use `#f6f6f6` or lighter.

You may want to use colors on your website to set the mood. There are varying ideas on the psychology of colors. So pick ones that work for you.

Designing your Website
to Use Less Energy

Avoid mixing similar colors, since they can be hard to distinguish. Don't rely solely on colors for anything. (8% of people (500 million) are color blind.)

Contrasting colors makes them more pleasing to the eye and easier for those who are colorblind to differentiate.

Tools for choosing color schemes include Adobe Color CC and Coolors.[137] You can also browse color schemes at OneXtraPixel, and at Color Combos[138] where you can click on a color to see combos using that color.

I also provide color scheme tools on my website – http://stubbart.com/computer_consulting/color_themes/.

---

[137] Adobe Color CC https://color.adobe.com; Coolors https://coolors.co/

[138] OneXtraPixel http://www.onextrapixel.com/2013/10/25/40-stunning-website-designs-with-great-color-schemes/; Color Combos http://www.colorcombos.com/popular-color-combinations

Chapter 6 – Print

The ideas in this chapter are more about saving paper and ink, than they are about saving energy. Though the less that is printed, the less energy is used by printers.

Causing printers to print more black or grey-scale and less color may save users money. Black Ink is less expensive than Colored Ink. But not all printers print black by using black ink or by using just black ink.

Applying these suggestions, will give you a better website presentation when users print a page from your website.

These suggestions are considered optional for Green Energy Websites.

You'll want your webpages to both display and print nicely. Use a print stylesheet `<link rel="stylesheet" type="text/CSS" media="print" href="print.css" />`.

If you're reducing load time by combining stylesheets, place your print styles within the `{}` of `@media print {}`. Place your `<link>` or `@media` for print last after your other styles.

Designing your Website to Use Less Energy

It is good to retest all your styles in your print styles to make sure they're set correctly for print. You can omit testing styles which are always `display:none`.

Don't forget to include those styles in your print stylesheet when you change your mind about not displaying that style.

If adding print CSS makes your stylesheet too big, minimize it. More info in Chapter 2 – Performance Step 6 – Lighten your CSS ***.

To save paper, use a smaller font-size. Also test with Print Preview rather than actually printing the page.

In my print stylesheet, I use the following font lists. These lists are created so that fonts which take less space are found first. This can save paper and ink.

Serif: `font-family: "Goudy Oldstyle", Garamond, "Baskerville Oldface", Baskerville, "Times New Roman", Times, serif;`

Sans-serif: `font-family: Evergreen139, "Arial Narrow", Tahoma, "Trebuchet MS", "Gill Sans", "Gill Sans MT", Arial, sans-serif;`

Cursive: `font-family: Evergreen,"Bradley Hand ITC","Lucida Handwriting","Monotype Corsiva","Brush Script MT",cursive;`

Reduce image size and `font-size` to make the image fit width-wise on one page.

Consider changing long floating divs to `float:none`.

---

[139] Evergreen is a font which was provided free by GreenPrint who designed that font to save ink. It is now available at a price from Fonts.com.

Chapter 6 – Print

To create a print stylesheet, I copy my regular stylesheet to `print.css`. Then I go through each style, making the following changes.

- Change background color to transparent if set
  ```
  background-color: transparent;
  ```
- Set font-size to 88% using percentage or hardcoding it
  ```
  font-size:88%;
  ```
- Override font list with one of the font lists above.
  My `html, body` specification is as follows:
  ```
  html, body {
  color: black;
  background-color: transparent;
  max-width: 100%;
  font-size:88%;
  font-family: "Goudy Oldstyle", Garamond,
  "Baskerville Oldface", Baskerville, "Times New
  Roman", Times, serif;
  }
  ```

I change `<h1>` to automatically page-break if needed. This does not save paper, but makes you're print look nicer. You may want to set the style for `<h2>` to break automatically, if you only have one `<h1>` and multiple `<h2>`.

If you're not already reducing the top or bottom margins on your headings, you may want to do so when printing.
```
h1 {
page-break-before: auto;
font-family: Evergreen, "Arial Narrow", Tahoma,
"Trebuchet MS", "Gill Sans", "Gill Sans MT", Arial,
sans-serif;
margin-bottom: -.25em;
}
```

I also add the following styles which are only for printing.
`.page_break` allows me to force a page_break anywhere.
`.no_print` allows me to not print certain elements.

Designing your Website
to Use Less Energy

```
.page_break    {
page-break-before: always;
padding-top: 25px;
}
.no_print {
display:none;
}
```

I also simplify hr and other elements which I display with images or which would otherwise take a lot of ink to print.

You may want higher resolution images to print. You display images should have a resolution of 72 pixels. Your print images should have a resolution of 150 to 300 pixels for better clarity – the smaller the resolution, the faster it will print.
However, the better the resolution, the more ink it takes to print the image.

If your image is displayed with
```
<img class="print_image" src="img_res72.jpg"
alt="My Image" />
```
Use this code in your regular stylesheet:
```
.print_image {}
```
Use this code in your print stylesheet to print a higher resolution image:
```
.print_image img {display:none;}
.print_image:after {content:url(print-logo.png); }
```

You may also want to flatten your image by changing it to an ink outline, if you have an image editor which gives you that option.
And/or you may want to save a greyscale version for printing to try to print with black ink.

You may be tempted to set the margin using @page in CSS. However, there is no standard minimum margin for

Chapter 6 – Print

printers. Users can set the margin and often can use fit-to-page.

You may also be tempted to set orientation to portrait using `@page`. But that option is often not supported.

I try to avoid these two temptations.

Designing your Website to Use Less Energy

Chapter 7 – Tips for Developers

General

Other things you can do to make your website use less energy include:

- Adding the 350 Challenge Badge[140] to your blog.

- Get your site Green Certified.[141]

- Suggest Carbon Offsets to your website visitors.

350 Challenge Badge: Adding the badge (and letting 350 Challenge know you've added the badge, results in them offsetting 350 pounds of carbon. They raise the money through ads.

Green Certified: This service costs $10/month.

---

[140] 350 Challenge Badge http://350.brighterplanet.com/
[141] Green Certified Site http://www.co2stats.com/

Chapter 7 – Tips for Developers

Carbon Offsets. You can suggest that your website visitors use these to offset their carbon emissions for travel, shipping, living, and surfing the web.

Native Energy, Carbonfund, CarbonFootprint, and TerraPass[142] all offer Carbon Offsets.

CarbonFootprint has an app you can place on your website.

---

[142] native energy http://www.nativeenergy.com/; Carbonfund https://www.carbonfund.org/; Carbon Footprint http://www.carbonfootprint.com/calculator.aspx; TerraPass http://www.terrapass.com/

Designing your Website
to Use Less Energy

Energy Saving Tips

You can place these energy saving tips on your website and use them yourself:

- Place your PC in PowerSaver Mode.
- Unplug your PC charger when your PC is turned off – or turn off the powerstrip it is plugged into.
- Dim the brightness of your screen. This can sometimes be done through buttons on your computer or keyboard; or alternatively through the control panel. Raymond.cc and softonic[143] suggest software you can download (often for free) to control the brightness and contrast of your screen.
- Take other energy saving options for your personal and business life like switching to 100% Green Power.
- Turn off wifi when not in use or at least reduce its range. The stronger the signal, the more energy it's using (probably minimal).
- Lower the volume on your pc or mute your speakers. Volumouse[144] software will change the

---

[143] Raymond.cc https://www.raymond.cc/blog/software-to-adjust-monitor-brightness-and-contrast-for-dell-studio-one-desktop/; softonic http://en.softonic.com/s/contrast-brightness-control
[144] Volumouse http://www.nirsoft.net/utils/volumouse.html

Chapter 7 – Tips for Developers

volume with a roll of the mouse wheel. You can control when the wheel changes volume and when it doesn't.

Designing your Website to Use Less Energy

Printing

Print Green. Reduce ink and paper use when printing, following the suggestions in the Print chapter.

Use Tree-Free paper.

Print using fit-to-page and double-sided when practical. Sometimes double-sided printing wastes paper because pages aren't lined up correctly or don't feed into printer correctly, unless you have automatic double-sided printing.
If you have automatic double-sided printing, make sure it flips the paper correctly depending on whether you're printing in portrait or landscape mode.

Use refilled ink cartridges.

Choose a green computer printer. Read my book A Greener Printer.
Things to consider:
- Xerox makes the ColorCube which is designed for printing color and uses non-toxic vegetable based ink in the shape of crayons. The crayons are different shapes for different models of the ColorCube and can't be interchanged. You may need to order this

printer directly from Xerox. The Xerox ColorCube was designed with the environment in mind.

- Epson and HP sell SuperTank Inkjet printers which come loaded with 2 years of ink (for 4000 pages). When the ink runs out, the tank can be refilled with liquid ink. Look for linseed oil, soy, or vegetable-based inks. Linseed oil inks dry faster than Soy or Vegetable based inks (except for the Xerox ColorCube) and therefore need less drying agents, if any.
- Soy ink filled laser cartridges are available from inkpal and Soy Print.[145] (These may still have toxic drying agents, but they don't contain petroleum-based ink).
- Non-toxic ink is available for printing presses (also called lithographic printers or offset printers) which can be messy, time consuming, and expensive. Printing Presses assume you will be printing 100,000 pages or more per month.
- What's the Energy Star Rating of your printer?[146] HP and Epson both make energy saving printers. Other companies make energy saving printers. But HP and Epson are the most popular.
- HP Inkjet cartridges contain print heads. Epson Inkjet cartridges do not. This makes Epson Inkjet

---

[145] inkpal http://www.inkpal.com/; Soy Print http://www.soyprint.net/

[146] Printer and Multifunction Device Energy Star Ratings http://www.energystar.gov/productfinder/product/certified-imaging-equipment/results?scrollTo=0&search_text=&sort_by=brand_name&sort_direction=asc&product_type_filter=Multifunction+Devices+%28MFD%29&product_type_filter=Printers&brand_name_isopen=&marking_technology_isopen=&markets_filter=United+States&page_number=0&lastpage=0

Designing your Website
to Use Less Energy

cartridges easier to refill, recycle, and to find a generic replacement for.

- Laser ink cartridges are more toxic than Inkjet cartridges. This is due to the drying agents which are present in both types of cartridges, but those in laser ink cartridges are more toxic. Laser printers also heat the ink to dry it, this releases more of the toxic chemicals into the air. This may not a problem for most people, but if you're sensitive to those things, it's something to consider. Also, less-toxic is better for the environment. Inkjet printers use less energy than laser printers.
- Spend more money and buy a printer which automatically double-sides.
- HP offers PVC-free models – other printer companies may also offer PVC-free models.
- Printer brands besides HP and Epson include Xerox, Brother, Lexmark, Samsung, Dell, Panasonic, and Ricoh.
- There are specialty printers available from a variety of companies for printing labels, photos, and textiles. The paper which labels and photos are printed on is usually not non-toxic or tree-free. Cork paper is available which has a backing. The backing might jam up your regular paper due to the glue heating up as it goes through the printer. It might be possible to use it in a label printer.

Chapter 7 – Tips for Developers

Shipping

If you ship items, use a green Shipping Company. The major shipping companies USPS, UPS, Fedex, and DSL are green in that order, with UPS and Fedex being about tied.

If you ship locally consider a bicycle shipping company if you have that option.

Designing your Website to Use Less Energy

Appendix A

Remove unused CSS classes from stylesheet

This script only works in Firefox. It displays the classes used on a webpage in one column on your webpage. It displays the classes used in your CSS file in a second column, so you can compare.

Place the script where you want the classes displayed.

Remove the script before uploading your webpage.

```
<script>
//get styles from html (webpage)
var htmlTags =
document.body.getElementsByTagName('*');
var htmlclassNames = {};
for (var i = 0; i <= htmlTags.length-1; i++) {
  var tag = htmlTags[i];
  if (tag.className) {
    var htmlclasses = tag.className.split(" ");
    for (var j = 0; j < htmlclasses.length; j++){
      var k = htmlclasses[j];
      if (! htmlclassNames[k]) {
        htmlclassNames[k] = true;
      }
    }
  }
}
var htmlclassList = [];
for (var name in htmlclassNames)
htmlclassList.push(name);
htmlclassList.sort();
a=htmlclassList.join('<br>');
```

Appendix A

```
   // get styles from first stylesheet
   var stylerules = [];
   var styleruleList =
document.styleSheets[0].cssRules;
   for (var i = 0; i <= styleruleList.length-1; i ++)
{
   //Note selectorText may contain multiple values,
you should split it up first and test each one
   //Also may get multiple occurrences of same class,
if class listed multiple times in stylesheet
     if (styleruleList[i].selectorText &&
styleruleList[i].selectorText.charAt(0) == '.') {

stylerules.push(styleruleList[i].selectorText);
     }
   }
   stylerules.sort();
   b=stylerules.join('<br>');
   b=b.replace(/\./g, '');
   document.write('<table><tr><td
valign="top">'+a+'</td><td
valign="top">'+b+'</td></tr></table>');
   </script>
```

Designing your Website
to Use Less Energy

About the Author

Dale Stubbart has worked with Computers for over 40 years. My Computer Consulting services include Websites. computer training, computer organization, data migration, data research, etc.

I do internet research, often quickly finding what others can't find or at least what they can't find quickly.

You can find out more information about my Computer Consulting Services at https://stubbart.com.

Who Wrote This Anyway?

Who Wrote This Anyway?

Dale Stubbart and his wife live in *Paradise*; that is providing they haven't forgotten for the moment where that is or what that's like. We try to allow ourselves to be happy and not get too bogged down by fear.

I was headed down the road to *Misery*, rather than the one to *Paradise*. However, something went awry and I kept being reminded of who I was and where I belonged. When I'm back here in *Paradise*, I can help others recall what's really important.

I'm help others Transition their Dreams and Visions. I walk with people into the dream state where fairies, angels, bumblebees, whatever, help bring their dreams to life. I draw on my experience with Spirit, Earth, Stories, and Tech to help people transform their lives and thus the world.

The Writing Muse found a willing partner in me for 90+ Titles. I can help you get your book self-published too. As an Author, I write stories in many genres or categories.

Dale Stubbart
Stubbart.com

Designing your Website to Use Less Energy

Often my stories include several genres. *Romance* often accompanies *Fantasy*. And one is a *Western Sci-Fi*.

You'll find humor and romance in many of my books. I keep them clean, non-formulaic, and happy. Many of my books include poetry. Sometimes I include phrases and words from languages other than English. Yet they're still easy to read, even my reference books.

My books are far from boring, as my narrators and others have confirmed. To help in that regard, I keep my books concise, yet complete. As my wife says, I'm the only person she knows who can write a novel in a page. That may be a slight exaggeration.

I write stories I like to read. You'll find yourself right smack dab in the midst of the story and have an enjoyable journey all the way through.

All of my books are on my website – Stubbart.com. The search box works very well.

My *Spiritual* books include Spiritual Reference, Mystical Writings, Spiritual Fiction, and Fiction with a Spiritual Theme. I write these with my self=friend *Yellow Bear*.

My *Earthwise* books include books for Living with Multiple Chemical Sensitivities, books about Energy-Wise Transportation, and other Earthwise books to help you live according to your Earthwise lifestyle.

My *Computer* books are written to be easily understood, even if you have limited technical experience. In fact, about half of my computer books are non-technical in nature, especially my book about a Robot who falls in love.

My *Reference* books are informative. They are stories, not just data, facts, and figures. Delve into your preferred topic or choose to learn about something new. My *Reference* books include books on *Food/Nutrition*.

Who Wrote This Anyway?

I write Romance because I'm truly in love, just ask my wife. My *Romance* stories will speak to the true Romantic in you, the one who wants to love and to be loved.

Children are some of my favorite people, no matter how old they are. My *Children's* stories will speak to the child in you. Let that happy baby come alive!

With Fantasies anything can happen and in my *Fantasy* stories it often does. Cheer on these protagonists as they live their unimaginably real lives in their impossibly real worlds. Get ready to be surprised with delight.

Fiction allows me to write what could happen. My *Fiction* stories allow you to consider alternate possible outcomes. What would the world be like, if ...?

Outer Space, Aliens, Science Fiction intrigues me. These *Sci-Fi* stories will speak to the space-farer and voyager in you. New worlds are out there for you to discover.

I write Thrillers when I no longer want to run and hide. My *Horror* stories will help you face your fears. As Franklin Roosevelt said, "The only thing we have to fear is fear itself." And at times, it can scare the $#@! out of me!

There are basically two ways to get to Paradise. You can enter by facing your fears and pains and allow them to dissolve and be healed. Or you can enter through joy and beauty. You can rest assured that I will enter through joy and beauty 99 times out of 100. And when you're willing, I'll take you with me. *Paradise is waiting for you. What are you waiting for?*

So take a trip to Stubbart.com. Find out more about my books and my work with Dreams. I think you'll find something you'll like, or my name's not *Dale Stubbart*.

Designing your Website
to Use Less Energy

Dale & Terry Stubbart